The Right Job for You

An Interactive Career Planning Guide

Revised Edition

J. Michael Farr

The Right Job for You, Revised Edition

An Interactive Career Planning Guide

©1991, 1997 by J. Michael Farr

Published by **JIST Works, Inc.**
720 N. Park Avenue
Indianapolis, IN 46202-3431
Phone: 317-264-3720 Fax: 317-264-3709 E-mail: JISTWorks@AOL.com

Other Books by J. Michael Farr

The Very Quick Job Search, 2nd Edition
The Quick Resume & Cover Letter Book
The Quick Interview & Salary Negotiation Book
Getting the Job You Really Want, 3rd Edition
How to Get a Job Now!
The Work Book
America's Fastest Growing Jobs, 4th Edition
America's Top Jobs™ for College Graduates, 2nd Edition
America's Top Jobs™ for People Without College Degrees, 3rd Edition
America's Top Medical, Education, & Human Services Jobs, 3rd Edition
America's Top Office, Management, Sales, & Professional Jobs, 3rd Edition
A Young Person's Guide to Getting and Keeping a Good Job

Interior Design by Debbie Berman

Printed in the United States of America

1 2 3 4 5 6 7 8 9   02 01 00 99 9897

We have been careful to provide accurate information throughout this book, but it is possible that errors and omissions have been introduced. Please consider this in making any career plans or other important decisions. Trust your own judgment above all else and in all things.

1-56370-286-X

P·R·E·F·A·C·E

As you enter the workforce, you can expect to spend about 40 years of your life working. That's about 80,000 hours (based on a 40-hour week). With each $10,000 of annual income, your lifetime earnings increase by $800,000. Other than personal relationships and values, your career choice probably is the most important decision you will make. Yet, if you are like most people, you probably spend more time buying clothes or planning meals in a month than you spend making important career planning decisions that will affect your entire life. Your ability to make good career-related decisions now and in the future will affect your earnings, lifestyle, personal satisfaction, and many other areas of life. It just makes sense to spend more time on this important issue.

This book will help you learn more about yourself—about the skills, accomplishments, and other life experiences that can help define what sorts of jobs you might do well. It also will help you define what kinds of people you like to work with, the salary range you want, and many other factors important in identifying your ideal job. You will find information on major occupational clusters—and specific jobs within each—that most closely match your interests and preferences. We'll also review training and educational options that will help you achieve your career goals. Chapter 7 shows you a process for making good career and life decisions.

It's important to know more about yourself when you are choosing a job objective that matches your needs. This book can help you plan your career and educational goals by giving you good career and life planning skills you can use over and over throughout your entire life.

Mike Farr

Mike Farr

C·O·N·T·E·N·T·S

Why People Work

Why *do* people work? Most people would list money as a major reason for working. Obviously money is important: You need it to pay for food, housing, clothes, health care, education, and all the rest of life's expenses. With luck, there's some left over for a few luxuries as well.

Money is one reward you receive for putting in a day's work. But there can be other rewards, too, if you want them. Any activity is rewarding if you like doing it. It's more rewarding still if it draws on your special skills or talents and gives you feelings of pride and satisfaction.

Do you have a job now? Do you like your work? Are you earning up to your full potential? If you answered "No" to any of these questions, this book can help. You need this book if:

▼ you're still searching for the "right" job;

▼ you're ready to make a job or career change;

▼ you're preparing to enter the workforce;

▼ you've been out of the workforce and are planning to return.

There are at least two other kinds of people who will benefit from this book:

▼ those who know what they want to do, and

▼ those who don't.

You Have to Learn to Change

Recent years have seen rapid changes in our economy and astonishing advances in technology. The ability to keep pace with these changes and locate good jobs is a valuable skill in itself.

New technology creates new jobs and changes old ones. Some jobs disappear or have far fewer people working in them than in the past. People need to keep learning new skills just to keep the jobs they have now.

Not surprisingly, these trends have produced another one: People change *careers* an average of five to seven times in the course of their working years. They change *jobs* even more than that. Sometimes a change occurs by choice, but sometimes people have no say in the matter at all. For whatever reason, their jobs are gone (or have changed so that they no longer want them). You can count on this happening to you at some time in your working life—at least once, if not quite a few times.

Who Needs This Book?

These rapid changes mean that good career planning is more important than ever. Good career planning can result in higher pay and better jobs. And it can help you find a career or job that is more satisfying to you.

So who needs this book? You do. Your friends do. Your neighbors, co-workers, and relatives do. Anyone who wants to find work, wants to enjoy work, or wants to keep working will benefit from this book.

What You'll Learn in This Book

Here is a quick review of what you'll learn in *The Right Job for You*. The book is divided into eight chapters. This chapter introduces the major topics of the book and gives you some things to think about.

Chapter 2 helps you define your skills and uncover hidden ones. Once you become aware of them, your skills can open the door to new career possibilities. Gaining a clear picture of your skills gives you a solid basis for making decisions about jobs. This may seem obvious, but a surprising number of people search for jobs without really knowing their skills or without knowing which ones they prefer to use every day on a job.

Chapter 3 helps you gather information about yourself to develop a personal "database." The exercises in this chapter will help you discover interests, strengths, and activities you might have overlooked. A personal database gives you a way to organize details about your life that can help in making decisions about your career options. It also helps you present yourself to potential employers with confidence and clarity, which gives you a competitive edge in the pool of job seekers.

In Chapter 4, you'll learn how to define your ideal job situation. You'll consider such things as hours, earnings, and location. The more you know about the job you want, the better your chances of finding work tailor-made for you. This information will also help you avoid jobs that are not right for you.

Chapter 5 shows you how to develop a specific career or job objective. You'll find information about the different career categories, or clusters, and details on more than 200 different jobs. More than 80 percent of all workers are employed in one of these jobs. This chapter also will help you match the information you've gathered about yourself to the careers that suit you best.

Chapter 6 gives an overview of the kinds of training and education available to prepare for an occupation. It's wise to consider the preparation a job requires before you make career decisions. Many of the better-paying jobs require special training or education that lasts from a few months to many years. This can be expensive and time-consuming, but knowing where and how to find information on financial assistance might just open possibilities you hadn't considered before.

In Chapter 7 you'll find a step-by-step approach to making decisions. You can use these techniques to make choices concerning your career, or for any other decision you face, big or small, now and in the future. Making major decisions can be overwhelming, especially ones about occupational and lifestyle choices. The strategy presented here helps you make good decisions based on your needs and desires. Having good decision-making skills greatly increases your chances of making good long-term career and life plans.

Finally, Chapter 8, offers tips for people in special situations. People at different life stages or in various situations have special issues to consider, and this chapter can help.

How to Use This Book

This book was designed to be *used*, not just read. There are helpful checklists, charts, and exercises throughout to help you learn, practice new skills, organize information, and make decisions.

You probably will find it best to review each chapter from beginning to end, doing each activity as you go. This will take longer than simply reading the book, but it is essential for you to get the most from it.

The Right Job for You is really a book about self-discovery. It not only helps you determine a job objective and make career plans but it helps you better understand your unique strengths, skills, and values. This self-knowledge is valuable for all lifestyle choices as well as for career-related ones.

This is *your* book. Write in it. Make notes in the margins. Make it your own.

Identify Your Skills

Employers surveyed over the years have reported that more than 90 percent of the job applicants they interview cannot explain their skills. Although job seekers may have the skills they need to do the job, they can't communicate them! One of the most important things you can do before deciding on or changing your career is to identify your skills. Then you will be able to emphasize the most valuable ones to an employer.

Identifying the skills you do best *and* enjoy using is a winning combination for career success. To help you do that, we'll work through a variety of exercises, examples, and worksheets. But before we begin, let's look at several possible definitions of the word *skill*.

Definition 1: A Skill Is Something You Can Do

True enough. Each of us could demonstrate many skills. These kinds of skills relate to *performance*, such as riding a bicycle or baking a cake. In turn, most of these skills can be broken down into smaller component skills that must be used together to do the more complex tasks. For example, balancing, pedaling, and steering are all component skills that enable you to ride a bike.

Baking a cake seems simple enough, but only if you have some of these component skills:

▼   shopping for ingredients

▼   reading a cookbook

▼   following directions

▼   organizing a work area

▼   using measuring cups and other tools

▼   using timing devices

▼   using an oven properly

In turn, each of these skills can be broken down further. For example, in order to use an oven, you have to be able to read the numbers or words on the dial and turn the dial, which requires fine motor coordination. You get the point. If you analyze any task carefully—even those that seem simple—more skills are required than you might think. Let's look at another definition of *skill*.

Definition 2: A Skill Is Something You Can Do Well

Being skillful at something means you do it well. Even if you can't bake a good cake, you might have some of the basic skills required to do so (reading a cookbook and following directions, for example). With experience, you can use skills you already have to learn new ones. So this definition has limits, too. Let's try again.

Definition 3: A Skill Is Something You Own

This is also true. For example, some people just seem to be organized. Other people just seem to get along well with others or have leadership abilities. Still others might be creative thinkers or good writers. These skills are more abstract than riding a bike or baking a cake, and it may be difficult to say just how they were learned. Still, they are real and important skills.

How Many Skills Do You Have?

Case Study: George

I met George several years ago in a workshop I was leading. He had been unemployed for a long time. When I asked George to tell me what he was good at, he couldn't think of a single thing! I asked him a few questions and found out that he had worked as a cabinet-maker for the same company for more than 15 years. He had never missed a day of work and had been late only once. He took pride in his work and had one of the lowest reject rates in his department of more than 20 people. No skills?

We've seen that a skill can be defined in many ways. Most people don't realize that everyone has hundreds of skills, not just a few. When I ask people what skills they have, too often they can't think of any, like George in the case study.

"No-Skills" Syndrome

Young people often underestimate their skills in the same way George did. So do women who have been "just a homemaker" with "no work experience." So do men and women who have had responsible and well-paying professional jobs. Over the years, I've talked with countless job seekers with "no-skills" syndrome; in fact, they have many more skills than they realize.

Many job seekers define skills like this:

▼   Special job-related abilities that require lots of training and/or experience and that an employer wants to pay money for, but that I don't have.

This common belief of having no skills is very discouraging. But it is not true. These job seekers do have skills—lots of them— and so do you.

"No-Skills" Syndrome Cure

One of the causes of "no-skills" syndrome is a lack of self-esteem. It happens to almost everyone who becomes unemployed, and it's common for even happily employed people to lack self-confidence occasionally. Another part of the problem is a lack of information about skills: what they are and how to identify them. Yet another problem is the lack of a skills language. If you can't describe what you do well, you might think you can't do anything well. Take heart. These are problems we can and will solve. Read on!

Three Types of Skills

This book was written to help you identify your skills and communicate them clearly to possible employers. Because skills can be defined in so many ways, systems for categorizing them are helpful. I will discuss one of the most useful systems for job seekers.

Simple skills, such as closing your fingers to grasp a pen (which is actually a very complex operation involving nerves and muscles), are building blocks for higher-level skills, such as writing a sentence, and for even more complex skills, such as writing a book.

To keep it simple, we'll divide skills into three major categories:

▼ Adaptive Skills/Good Worker Traits

▼ Transferable Skills

▼ Job Content Skills

Let's take a brief look at each category.

Adaptive Skills

These are the skills you use every day to survive and get along. They are called *adaptive skills* because they allow you to adapt or adjust to a variety of situations, including work. We could also call them *good worker traits*. Some of them can be considered part of our basic personalities. Two adaptive skills valued by most employers are getting to work on time and getting along well with others.

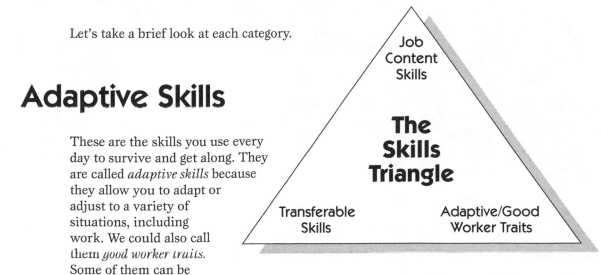

Job
Content
Skills

**The
Skills
Triangle**

Transferable
Skills

Adaptive/Good
Worker Traits

Transferable Skills

These are *general skills* that are useful in a variety of jobs and can be transferred from one job or career to another. For example, communication skills and organizational skills would be desirable in almost any job.

Job Content Skills

These skills are *related to a particular job or type of job.* They are the skills people usually think of when they are asked whether they have any skills. A secretary's job content skills might include being able to type quickly and accurately and use several word-processing programs. A carpenter's job content skills would include working with tools and making precise measurements.

There is some overlap between the three skills categories. Some skills could also be considered personality traits (for example, being trustworthy, dependable, or organized).

Which group of skills—adaptive, transferable, or job content—do you think is the most important to your job search? Rate the groups on the lines below, number 1 being the most important.

1. _____

2. _____

3. _____

Key Idea

If the employer feels you will not be dependable or won't get along well with co-workers, you will not be hired—even if you have the experience to handle the job.

How Employers See Your Skills

Most employers react within a few seconds to people they interview. If this initial reaction is negative, you probably will not be hired. Employers react first to your adaptive skills, including these:

▼   your dress and grooming

▼   your handshake

▼   your use of language

▼   whether you are on time

Adaptive Skills Make the Biggest Impression

Job seekers who can effectively present their adaptability to a new work situation often get jobs over people with more experience and training.

You may find that surprising, but it's true: It is often the better-prepared job seeker who gets the job, even if another applicant is more qualified. Why is this so? In an interview, an employer is looking for clues about what a person will be like on the job. And most people who are fired or lose their jobs do so because they can't adapt and get along—not because they can't do the job itself. In a survey of personnel directors from the 1,000 largest U.S. corporations, only 4 percent listed "not doing job" as the most disturbing employee behavior.[1]

The following table lists behaviors that can cause a person to lose a job. In this survey, responses related to actual job performance totaled only 32 percent. The remaining 68 percent related to poor adaptive skills. The most frequently noted problems were lying and dishonesty (14 percent), absenteeism and tardiness (12 percent), arrogance and overconfidence (10 percent), and lack of dedication (6 percent).

Transferable Skills Highlight Your Potential

Once you convince an employer you can adapt easily to a work situation, your transferable skills are next in importance. In most cases, your ability to learn the new job quickly will be more important than job-related experience. Most employers know you will have to be retrained in their system.

Your transferable and adaptive skills might be more important to an employer than someone else's knowledge of a specific procedure.

Key Idea

If an employer believes that you lack certain transferable or adaptive skills, someone with less experience may get the job.

Case Study: Pam

Pam Smith, who edited an early draft of the manuscript for this book, provides a good example of how much weight employers give to transferable and adaptive skills. In Pam's first attempt to get an advertising copy writing job, there were 60 other applicants. Most had more experience than she did.

Before the interview, Pam went to the library and checked out 20 books on the advertising business. When this came up in the interview, the employer was impressed with her transferable and adaptive skills: researching, creative problem-solving, and willingness to work hard to learn. She got the job.

Disturbing Employee Behaviors List

Behavior	Top Total (%)	Personnel Management (%)	Management (%)
Personal			
lying/dishonesty	14	16	12
ego problems/arrogance			
overconfidence/aggressiveness	10	20	—
lack of dedication or commitment			
or concern/not a team player	6	4	8
poor attitude	5	2	8
poor listener	5	6	4
not getting along well			
not communicating well with others	4	2	6
whining/complaining	4	2	6
negative attitude toward job or company	3	—	6
not utilizing full potential	3	2	4
laziness/no motivation/no enthusiasm	2	6	—
not looking at me/			
not looking me in the eye	3	2	4
excessive nervousness	2	2	2
not creative	2	4	—
lack of character/integrity	2	2	2
Absenteeism			
absenteeism	8	4	12
tardiness	4	4	4
Poor Work Habits			
not following instructions/			
not responding to instructions	5	8	2
not doing job	4	2	6
unproductivity/not accomplishing			
tasks/no follow-through	4	6	2
goofing off/personal business			
on work time	4	2	6
irresponsibility	4	4	4
unreliability/unpredictability/			
inconsistencies	4	4	4
not following company policy			
or procedures	3	2	4
making decisions without facts			
or with limited information	2	2	2
incompetence	2	4	—
don't know/no answer	8	6	10

Based on a survey of employers, giving the major reason for firing an employee.

Job Content Skills Are Important

Of course, job content skills *are* important, especially in certain technical or professional jobs. No matter how nice you are or how good you are with your hands (another transferable skill), you can't get a job as an airline pilot unless you know how to fly. (This is a comforting thought if you're a passenger.) There are many jobs like this, but there are even more that are not. I have read estimates that one-half of all the jobs in North America could be learned by adults of average ability in two weeks or less. To learn these jobs, workers would use their adaptive and transferable skills to make up for what they lacked in specific job knowledge and skills.

For this reason, I've put job content skills third in importance in the Skills Triangle. Even when specific job skills are required, an employer will probably hire the job seeker who makes the best impression. This is called *skills communication,* and you will master this as we go along.

The series of exercises that follow will help you identify your unique strengths in the Skills Triangle. We'll begin with adaptive skills.

Identify Your Adaptive Skills

I mentioned earlier that we all have hundreds of skills. As you read this, for example, you are using two valuable skills: reading and understanding written English. In your lifetime, you have acquired many skills that you must learn to recognize. You may consider some of them personality traits, but whatever you call them, they are important to your job search.

Your "Good Worker" Traits

Write *at least* five things about yourself that you think make you a good worker.

_____

_____

_____

_____

_____

_____

_____

_____

Of these, pick the three that you think are particularly important and write them below.

1. _____

2. _____

3. _____

These skills are probably your strongest ones—the ones you can best defend and the ones that are most true for you.

The Adaptive Skills Checklist

Adaptive skills are the *key skills* that are important to most employers. You should emphasize these if you have them.

Following is a list of adaptive skills, or good worker traits, that I've collected from groups who have participated in my workshops. This is not a complete list, and you may well come up with others that are not on it.

For each skill, check one of the boxes if you usually, sometimes, or only rarely use or display that skill.

Adaptive Skill	Usually	Sometimes	Rarely
Key Skills			
accept supervision	✓		
get along with co-workers	✓		
get things done on time	✓		
good attendance record	✓	✓	
honest	✓		
productive	✓	✓	
punctual	✓	✓	
work hard	✓	✓	
Other Skills			
ambitious	✓		
assertive	✓		
capable	✓		
cheerful	✓		
competent	✓		
complete assignments	✓		
conscientious	✓		
coordinator		✓	
creative thinker		✓	
dependable	✓		

Adaptive Skill	Usually	Sometimes	Rarely
discreet			
eager			
efficient			
energetic			
enthusiastic			
expressive			
flexible			
formal			
friendly			
good-natured			
helpful			
humble			
imaginative			
independent			
industrious			
informal			
intelligent			
intuitive			
learn quickly			
loyal			
mature			
methodical			
modest			
motivated			
natural			
open-minded			
optimistic			
original			
patient			
persistent			
physically strong			
practical			
problem solver			
proud of doing a good job			
reliable			
resourceful			
responsible			
self-confident			
sense of humor			
sincere			
spontaneous			
steady			
strong			
tactful			
tenacious			

Adaptive Skill	Usually	Sometimes	Rarely
thrifty			
trustworthy			
versatile			
well-organized			
willing to learn new things			
Any Other Skills			

Your Top Five Adaptive Skills

Now look at the list of "good worker" traits you compiled earlier in this chapter. Find the skills for which you checked *Usually* in the Adaptive Skills Checklist. Comparing both lists, write your top five adaptive skills in the space below.

1. _____

2. _____

3. _____

4. _____

5. _____

There, you sound pretty good! Employers look very hard at job seekers to determine whether they can be depended upon to do a good job. It's a basic employer expectation. If an employer doesn't think you are dependable, you won't be hired—even if you have great experience.

For example, a typist who types 100 words a minute but who appears to have a bad attitude won't be seriously considered over someone who types only 75 words a minute but appears pleasant, hardworking, and easy-going. If you don't have much work experience or you are changing fields, presenting your adaptive skills is very important.

Develop a Skills Language

Having a list of skills is a good starting point, but you must also get used to using a new skills language. With practice, you will find it natural to communicate your skills where it counts—in an interview. Knowing you have skills and being able to tell others about them also feels good!

Key Idea

Use any part of your life experience to support your ability to do something in a job. You can use anything you've done well.

Learn to Prove It

It's nice that you have these skills. But how can you convince someone else? One approach—called Prove It[2]—is to describe a situation in which you used the skill and did well. Read the following examples offered by a young man with limited work experience to show that he has the adaptive skill of being a dependable worker.

Good Examples of How to Prove It

Proof 1: "Over the past year, I have had an excellent attendance record, and I have always been on time, even when the weather was bad."

Proof 2: "Last summer, I ran a concession stand at the county fair and worked 12 hours a day. Because my cousin, who owns the concession, was ill, I did the work two people usually do."

Proof 3: "In high school, I repaired electronic equipment for all my friends. I was good enough to get assigned to the school's broadcasting program as the electronic equipment technician."

These proofs indicate an ability to be a dependable worker. To improve on these examples, the job seeker should use numbers and mention results. You gain a powerful impact when you describe activities in terms of number of units, percentage or dollar increases, and similar measurements. Now let's take a look at how this job seeker learned to improve his skills language.

Better Examples to Prove It

Proof 1: "Over the past three years, I have had a better attendance record than 90 percent of my classmates. In fact, the only time I was absent in the past year was when I had a fever of 103, and even then I missed only one day. I was on the school newspaper staff, and we never missed a deadline in my two years."

Proof 2: "Last summer my cousin became ill and could not run his concession at the county fair. Even though I had never run a concession before, I bought the supplies and handled all the details in time to open the stand on the first day—with only one day's notice. Two people usually run the stand, but I ran it myself without help. I served an increase of 36 percent over the previous year. Profits were up 50 percent because I bought supplies wholesale and in quantity. I worked 12-hour days but always opened on time."

Proof 3: "During high school, I spent a lot of my spare time reading anything on electronics and fixing equipment for friends. When I heard that the school's FM transmitter for the student-run radio station went down, I volunteered to fix it. I dug up schematics for it and figured out what was wrong. It took all night, but the station was back on the air the next day. From then on, I was the unofficial technician for the school's A/V and electronic equipment. I had most of the broken equipment working within a few months and kept it working during the three years I was there. Before I graduated, the principal told me I had saved them more than $9,000 in estimates they had gotten for electronic equipment repair and maintenance."

Do you see the difference between the first set of proofs and the second set?

Use Your Life Experiences to Help You Prove It

Lots of people think they can't "prove it" because they don't have experience. Not so. Don't confuse paid work experience with activities that show employers your skills.

For example, if you like to organize things at home, the odds are that you'll do the same on a job. Employers will hire you for your potential. What you've done in previous jobs is important (more so for some jobs than others), but your ability to adapt to and do well in their job is what employers want. If you give examples of how you have done well in the past, you will have a much better chance of getting a job offer over those who are more qualified technically.

Life Experiences You Can Use to Prove It

Look at the list of life experiences below. Take a moment to think about which of these experiences you have had. In the next chapter, you will develop a complete history using many of the sources on the following list for your proofs. Once you have done that, you'll be able to provide many examples from your background to support the skills you've chosen to emphasize in your job search.

▼ Activities you planned or organized

▼ Anything you do (or did) well

▼ Volunteer experience

▼ Part-time or summer jobs

▼ Church, charitable, political, or civic involvement

▼ Leisure activities

▼ Anything you did to make money

▼ School or training experience

▼ Successes or accomplishments

▼ Participation in sports or extracurricular activities

▼ Responsibilities (family or otherwise)

▼ And, lest we forget, any jobs you've had—including the military

More Examples to Prove It

Here are some more examples of Prove It:

Adaptive Skills: Responsible, Hardworking

Proof: "I am the oldest of six children. From the time I was 7 years old, I was responsible for caring for the younger ones, cooking three days a week, and doing chores. I'm used to hard work, and I like to stay busy,"

Adaptive Skills: Flexible, Trustworthy

Proof: "Over the past six years, I've had a variety of increasingly responsible positions. While in school, I opened and closed a store that had more than $800,000 in inventory, and I provided all supervision and customer service in the owner's absence. While in the military, I was responsible for a unit of more than 30 people and a civilian budget equivalent to more than $4 million per year."

Adaptive Skills: Reliable, Self-Motivated

Proof: "Over the past two years I have attended school full-time while holding down a 20-hour-a-week job. It hasn't been easy, but I haven't missed a day of either work or school. My grades are above average, and I've paid all my school expenses from savings and my income from my job."

Adaptive Skills: Self-Disciplined, Goal-Oriented, Motivated

Proof: "Although I am young and have not had many paid jobs, I do have work experience. For the past three years, I've practiced gymnastics three or four evenings a week, plus Saturdays and many Sundays, too. Even though I'm tired after a full day at school, I get there on time and push hard to get better. I am used to the discipline of a 12-hour day, and I have organized my time well enough to keep a B average. I now intend to put my full effort into doing well on my first job."

Now You Prove It!

Now it's your turn. Turn back to the list you made of your top five adaptive skills. For each of the five skills, pick three situations in which you used that skill. These might be from work, volunteer activities, home, recreation, school, or anywhere else. Write a brief description of each situation, including numbers and results. You might find it helpful to write these on a separate sheet first and then rewrite them here, including only the most important points.

Adaptive Skill 1: _____

Proof 1: _____

_____

_____

_____

Proof 2: _____

_____

_____

_____

Proof 3: _____

_____

_____

_____

Adaptive Skill 2: _____

Proof 1: _____

_____

_____

_____

Proof 2: _____

_____

_____

_____

Proof 3: _____

_____

_____

_____

Adaptive Skill 3: _____

Proof 1: _____

_____

_____

_____

Proof 2: _____

_____

_____

_____

Proof 3: _____

_____

_____

_____

Adaptive Skill 4: _____

Proof 1: _____

_____

_____

_____

Proof 2: _____

_____

_____

_____

Proof 3: _____

_____

_____

_____

Adaptive Skill 5: _____

Proof 1: _____

_____

_____

_____

Proof 2: _____

_____

_____

_____

Proof 3: _____

_____

_____

_____

Already, you are learning to present yourself better to an employer. By saying what you do well and proving it with examples, you are more convincing than the 90 percent of job seekers who have not done this exercise.

Identify Your Transferable Skills

While writing your own proofs earlier, you may have noticed that, as you were supporting one adaptive skill, you mentioned other skills in the proof you offered. To see how this works, let's go back again to the high school radio station example. In addition to dependability, the following skills popped out:

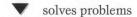 solves problems    learns quickly

▼ helps others   ▼ takes risks

▼ is frugal   ▼ handles responsibility

▼ cooperates   ▼ is dependable

▼ is willing to work long hours   ▼ works without supervision

▼ is self-motivated   ▼ meets deadlines

▼ is quality-minded   ▼ works under pressure

▼ takes pride in work   ▼ is helpful

All that with just a short story! In fact, if you present proof of one skill, it's hard to avoid showing you have others. Many of these skills can be used in a variety of jobs other than at a radio station. That makes them transferable skills.

Another example is that same young man's experience working at the concession stand. In addition to dependability, the following skills were demonstrated:

▼ handling money   ▼ selling things

▼ working under pressure   ▼ working hard

▼ meeting deadlines   ▼ managing time

▼ planning   ▼ being flexible

▼ organizing   ▼ showing responsibility

▼ being profit-minded   ▼ showing enterprise

▼ controlling costs   ▼ making decisions

▼ meeting customers   ▼ using good judgment

▼ solving problems   ▼ being energetic

There are a great many more such skills, and each person has a unique combination. Let's discover your unique skills.

The Transferable Skills Checklist

The following checklist was compiled to help you identify skills you might otherwise overlook. Take time to do this exercise thoroughly! For each skill, there are two columns. *Do Well:* Check this box if you are particularly good at using a skill. *Enjoy:* Check this box if you enjoy using a skill. Check both boxes if they both apply. The *Key Skills* on the list are ones that really impress employers. People with these skills tend to gain more responsible positions and higher pay.

Transferable Skill	Enjoy	Do Well
Key Skills		
communicate in writing		
instruct others		
manage money, budgets		
manage people		
meet deadlines		
meet the public		

21

Transferable Skill	Enjoy	Do Well
negotiate		
organize/manage projects		
speak in public		
Using My Hands/Dealing with Things		
assemble things		
build things		
construct/repair buildings		
drive, operate vehicles		
good with hands		
observe/inspect		
operating tools, machines		
repair things		
use complex equipment		
Dealing with Data		
check for accuracy		
classify things		
compare		
compile		
count		
evaluate		
investigate		
keep financial records		
locate answers, information		
manage money		
observe/inspect		
pay attention to details		
record facts		
research		
synthesize		
take inventory		
Working with People		
administer		
care for		
confront others		
counsel people		
demonstrate		
diplomatic		
firm		
get along with others		
help others		
instruct		
interview		
kind		
listen		

Transferable Skill	Enjoy	Do Well
mentoring		
negotiate		
patient		
persuade		
pleasant		
sensitive		
supervise		
tactful		
teach		
tolerate		
trust		
understand		

Using Words, Ideas

	Enjoy	Do Well
articulate		
communicate verbally		
correspond with others		
create new ideas		
design		
develop/create		
do research		
edit		
ingenious		
inventive		
remember information		
speak in public		
think logically		
write clearly		

Leadership

	Enjoy	Do Well
achieve results		
act decisively		
arrange social functions		
be competitive		
delegate		
direct others		
explain things		
have confidence		
influence others		
initiate new tasks		
make decisions		
manage or direct others		
mediate problems		
motivate others		
motivate self		
negotiate agreements		
plan		

Transferable Skill	Enjoy	Do Well
run meetings		
solve problems		
take risks		
Creative/Artistic		
create		
dance, move physically		
draw, paint, sculpt		
express emotions, thoughts		
perform, act		
present artistic ideas		
Other Skills		

Your Top Ten Transferable Skills

Now go back over your list and select the ten skills you think are the best ones for you to use in your next job. Consider including skills you feel strongly about even if you are not sure just how you could get paid for using them. In no particular order, list your ten top transferable skills.

1. _____

2. _____

3. _____

4. _____

5. _____

6. _____

7. _____

8. _____

9. _____

10. _____

Once Again, Prove It!

Now that you've sorted out your ten best transferable skills, it's time to support them, just as you did in the adaptive skills exercises. (Remember, you are still developing your skills language.)

The following are some examples of how several people used their life experiences as proof of transferable skills.

▼ making homemade bread with my kids

▼ building a tree house by myself when I was 12 years old

▼ helping to organize the Junior Class Bash in high school

▼ reducing customer complaints by more than 30 percent while increasing sales by more than 35 percent in one year

▼ getting through school with good grades while working part-time (Whew!)

Identify Your Successes

With these examples in mind, think of at least five situations in which you did something well and enjoyed doing it. These can be situations in which you felt successful, even if you won no awards or received no special recognition. In the spaces below, jot down enough of each experience to remind you what it was. Try to include at least one situation from childhood, another from high school, and the rest from whenever you want. The successes can be related to work, hobbies, recreation, volunteer work, a special project, or something else.

Success 1: _____

_____

Success 2: _____

_____

Success 3: _____

_____

Success 4: _____

_____

Success 5: _____

_____

_____

25

Describing Your Successes

Now you can expand on your successful experiences by describing them in detail. Use a separate sheet of paper for each story. Name the experience, then write as much as you can remember about it. Write it just as you would tell it—don't be concerned about your writing style. Look at the Real Success Story that follows as an example.

A Real Success Story

Note: This is adapted from a story presented in a workshop years ago. It's an example of how even a small incident can be a big success.

"It's hard for me to think of anything recent that's an outstanding success, so I'll use something small. I'm a homemaker with three children, and two are under 5 years old. Yesterday was a rainy day, so I wanted something fun to keep them occupied. I've been making homemade bread every week or so for the past year. It's good food and provides a sort of relaxation for me. I usually start the bread when the kids are taking a nap. In the afternoon, I knead it, and that always relaxes me somehow. It feels good, and I know it helps the family share in something I've created.

"Yesterday I let the kids help. They enjoyed the responsibility and were very proud of their work. The day seemed short, and I felt the project was a success. I enjoyed doing it."

Memory Joggers for Your Success Stories

▼ What happened?

▼ What was your role in it?

▼ Who else was involved and did that make a difference to you?

▼ What did you particularly like about what you did?

▼ Where did it happen? Did that have something to do with liking it?

▼ Why did you pick this as a success?

For each success, you should write at least a page with as many details as you can remember. This exercise should take about 60 to 90 minutes to complete. Save these sheets for later reference.

What Were the Ingredients of Your Success?

Once you have written the story of each of your successes, the next step is to review each story and identify the skills you used. Circle any skill words or personality traits you included. If you used a skill but didn't include the word in your story, write that skill in the margin.

It's easy to find ten or more skills in each of your stories. If you can't find at least ten, maybe you need help recognizing your skills. (For practice, look at the concession stand example again. For instance, how did all that equipment get set up and operating? How did the person find out how to contact suppliers?)

Transferable Skills Summary

Go back to the list of your top ten transferable skills. Transfer that list to the left column that follows.

Next, review your success stories and, in the right column below, compile a list of the top ten skills you've identified in those stories (the skills you circled and those written in the margins.)

Top Ten Transferable Skills	Skills from Success Stories
1. _____	1. _____
2. _____	2. _____
3. _____	3. _____
4. _____	4. _____
5. _____	5. _____
6. _____	6. _____
7. _____	7. _____
8. _____	8. _____
9. _____	9. _____
10. _____	10. _____

Some skills appear on both lists. What does that mean to you?

Your Most Important Transferable Skills

The next several exercises will help you narrow down your lists of transferable skills to the ones that are most valuable to you in your job search. First, choose your top ten skills from the two lists you just completed. List your choices in no particular order.

1. _____

2. _____

3. _____

4. _____

5. _____

6. _____

7. _____

8. _____

9. _____

10. _____

Set Priorities with the Forced Choice Grid

Every possible combination of numbers 1 through 10 is included in the Forced Choice Grid below. Each number refers to one of the top ten transferable skills you listed. Compare each skill to its pair and, for each combination, select the skill you would choose if you could only use one of them in your work. Circle that number.

For example, let's say you listed *organized* as skill 1 above and *good with numbers* as skill 2. You would now ask yourself, "In my next job, would I rather use my organizational skills or my skill with numbers?" Circle the number representing your preferred skill of the two and go on to the next pair until you have worked through the entire grid.

Forced Choice Grid

1	2																
1	3	2	3														
1	4	2	4	3	4												
1	5	2	5	3	5	4	5										
1	6	2	6	3	6	4	6	5	6								
1	7	2	7	3	7	4	7	5	7	6	7						
1	8	2	8	3	8	4	8	5	8	6	8	7	8				
1	9	2	9	3	9	4	9	5	9	6	9	7	9	8	9		
1	10	2	10	3	10	4	10	5	10	6	10	7	10	8	10	9	10

Now add up how many times you circled each number in the grid and write the totals below:

1. _____ 3. _____ 5. _____ 7. _____ 9. _____

2. _____ 4. _____ 6. _____ 8. _____ 10. _____

Your Priorities: Results of the Forced Choice Grid

What does the Forced Choice Grid tell you about your priorities? On the first line of the left column that follows, write the number of the skill that turned up most often on the grid. On the next line of the "Number" column, write the number of the next most frequent skill, and so forth. In the "Skill" column on the right, write the name of the skill that corresponds to the number.

Number	Skill
_____	_____
_____	_____
_____	_____
_____	_____
_____	_____
_____	_____

Are there any surprises in the way you prioritized your skills? Sometimes our sense of what is most important differs from the result of a careful analysis. This is your list, and if you want to rearrange the order of it, trust your instincts.

Your Top Five: The Best of the Best

Now it's time to narrow down your list of the most important transferable skills to the top five. These are the most important ones to keep in mind in your job search. The work you've done in this section points to these skills as major factors in your success and satisfaction as a worker.

1. _____
2. _____
3. _____
4. _____
5. _____

Why Adaptive and Transferable Skills Are Important

Your adaptive and transferable skills are part of what makes you unique. This is one reason they are more important than job content skills to you as a person and as a job seeker. Although these skills may change over time, what usually happens is that some skills continue to develop more than others.

You are likely to change jobs *and to change careers* often. Your ability to transfer your skills and adapt to a new career is very important. Even if you don't want or plan to change careers, you might be forced to. Technology is changing so rapidly that many current jobs will be gone within 10 or 20 years. People who have a good understanding of their strong adaptive and transferable skills will make job and career changes more smoothly and successfully than others. Employers are impressed by job seekers who know their strengths and who can communicate and use them.

Not to Be Forgotten: Your Job Content Skills

Stressing the importance of adaptive and transferable skills in the job search does not mean that specific job-related skills are not important. They are. Many jobs require specific job-related skills gained from training, education, or experience. For example, a secretary *does* need to know how to type, and a brain surgeon *certainly* needs to have more specific skills than being good with his or her hands.

Most employers won't interview people for jobs if they don't have the essential, entry-level, job-related skills or credentials for that job. A secretary who can't type has a problem. And you really do need to have a medical degree and certification to do brain surgery in this country. (Thank goodness!) But many people get jobs over people who are "better qualified" because they do well in the interview. They convince the employer that they can overcome their lack of credentials with superior adaptive and transferable skills.

So in this section, list the important job-related skills you have, even if you don't think you can (or want to) use them in your next job. These are skills you gained through previous training, education, hobbies, leisure activities, family responsibilities, or other sources.

In the two columns below, list skills you gained in previous jobs in the left column and skills gained from education and training in the right column.

Identify Your Job Content Skills

Previous Job Content Skills	Job Content Skills from Education/Training
1. _____	1. _____
2. _____	2. _____
3. _____	3. _____
4. _____	4. _____
5. _____	5. _____
6. _____	6. _____

7. _____   7. _____

8. _____   8. _____

9. _____   9. _____

10. _____   10. _____

These lists show your job content skills at this moment. As you decide on a career objective, you will be able to describe the job content skills and training you need to acquire.

Your Top Five Job Content Skills

List below the five most important job content skills you have right now. Are these the ones you want to use in your next job? By the time you finish this book, you should have an easier time answering that question.

1. _____

2. _____

3. _____

4. _____

5. _____

Chapter 2 Endnotes

1. From a survey conducted by Burke Marketing Research and presented in Robert Half's *Robert Half-Hiring* (New York: Crown Publishers).

2. Bernard Haldane suggests giving specific examples of how skills were used as a way to prove them in an interview. He authored *Career Satisfaction and Success* (Indianapolis: JIST Works).

3
chapter

Develop Your Personal Database

The typical job interview lasts less than an hour. If you're going to make a fool of yourself, you will probably do it in the first few minutes of chitchat: "Lovely day today, isn't it?" you say brightly, and the interviewer responds, "Well, I guess so, if you like rain." But if you get through the first few minutes without disaster, what do you do next?

Organize Your Personal History

To be prepared for whatever comes next in an interview, you must review your personal history. Give particular attention to what might interest the employer. Because you have years of life history but less than 60 minutes in an interview, it is wise to prepare ahead of time:

▼ Know what information an employer may want.

▼ Get this information organized in advance.

This chapter helps you organize your life into a kind of database. You can use this database throughout your job search. *Database* is a computer term that describes details you can't remember all the time but know how to retrieve if you need them. I use the term in this book to refer to all the information about yourself that might support your job search.

The Uses of a Personal Database

▼ To help you define a career direction or job objective

▼ To help you avoid jobs you are not likely to enjoy or do well

▼ To help you learn from past mistakes

▼ To give you clues from volunteer work, hobbies, and other activities that you can use in career planning

▼ To prepare you to be more relaxed in interviews (because you will have done your homework)

The database you build is an important tool. You will use it to select a specific job objective, fill out applications, construct resumes, answer tough interview questions, and develop many other job-search skills.

Build Your Database

The exercises in this chapter are designed to help you develop confidence in your unique strengths. They group your skills into the following categories:

▼ hobbies and recreational activities

▼ family experiences ,

▼ education

▼ extracurricular activities

▼ military and technical training

▼ conferences, workshops, and seminars

▼ college and beyond

▼ volunteer and work history

Obviously, not everybody has experience in all of these categories. As you go through this chapter, keep in mind that these exercises are designed to build your confidence and your awareness of your unique strengths. They are not meant to make you feel inadequate. If you can't think of any recreational activities you've engaged in, if you have never volunteered for anything or never had a paying job, don't be discouraged. We all have to start somewhere.

If, however, you have lots of experience, feel free to use additional sheets of paper to do the exercises. Then select the experiences that are most relevant to your current career interests.

Hobbies and Recreational Activities

Think about any hobbies or recreational activities you've been involved in. Most likely you pursued them because you enjoyed them. Some of these you enjoyed as a child and have since abandoned; others are part of your life now. These could include collecting things, traveling, taking pictures, making things, catching turtles, reading, or playing sports. Complete the following worksheets, taking the time to do each one thoroughly. Use additional paper as needed.

List Your Hobbies and Activities

Step 1: Remembering

List all of your hobbies or recreational activities—past and present—here:

_____   _____

_____   _____

_____   _____

_____   _____

_____   _____

_____   _____

_____   _____

Step 2: Selecting

Circle the five activities from your list of hobbies and recreational activities that were the most rewarding or fun. Of the five, select at least one that you did only as a kid and another that you did for a longer time.

Step 3: Analyzing

For each of the five activities you chose, answer the following.

Activity 1: _____

Why did you pick this as one of your five favorite activities? _____

_____

What special things made this meaningful for you? _____

_____

_____

_____

What skills were you using? _____

_____

_____

Which of these skills would you like to use in your next job?

_____

_____

Activity 2: _____

Why did you pick this as one of your five favorite activities? _____

_____

What special things made this meaningful for you? _____

_____

What skills were you using? _____

_____

_____

Which of these skills would you like to use in your next job?

_____

_____

Activity 3: _____

Why did you pick this as one of your five favorite activities? _____

_____

What special things made this meaningful for you? _____

_____

What skills were you using? _____

_____

_____

Which of these skills would you like to use in your next job?

_____

_____

Activity 4: _____

Why did you pick this as one of your five favorite activities? _____

_____

What special things made this meaningful for you? _____

_____

What skills were you using? _____

_____

Which of these skills would you like to use in your next job?

_____

_____

Activity 5: _____

Why did you pick this as one of your five favorite activities? _____

_____

What special things made this meaningful for you? _____

_____

What skills were you using? _____

_____

_____

Which of these skills would you like to use in your next job?

_____

_____

What Skills Do You Use the Most?

In the spaces provided, write the skills that you listed for each of the five activities. If you noted a skill more than once, put a check mark by it for each time it is repeated.

_____   _____

_____   _____

_____ _____

_____ _____

_____ _____

_____ _____

_____ _____

_____ _____

_____ _____

Step 4: The Final Five

From the list of skills you just made, select the five you would most like to use in your next job. Pay special attention to any skill that has one or more check marks beside it. List the top five below:

1. _____

2. _____

3. _____

4. _____

5. _____

Family Experiences

This set of worksheets asks you to recall activities from your childhood and to consider the responsibilities you take on at home now. It's so easy to take things for granted that you probably overlook many significant skills—skills that just might have career potential.

Childhood

Some people have substantial responsibilities while growing up: caring for other family members, working in a family business (a farm counts), or performing regular and important chores. An example of how people overlook these responsibilities can be seen in the following case study.

Step 1: Remembering

Write significant family chores you had up to the age you moved away from your family's home:

_____

_____

_____

_____

_____

_____

_____

Adulthood

As any homemaker knows, taking care of children and providing for a family are not easy tasks. In fact, many authorities now agree that homemaking is a job, even if you don't get paid for it. If you worked, went to school, or did some other significant activity while handling family responsibilities, consider it an important accomplishment. This applies to both men and women, although women more typically have careers as homemakers. Complete the exercises that follow if they relate to your family responsibilities either as a child or as an adult.

Step 1: Remembering

List all the major family tasks for which you are responsible as an adult:

_____

_____

_____

_____

_____

_____

Case Study: Louis

Louis was a 22-year-old about to graduate from a computer programming course. We were discussing job histories, and he told me he had never had a job. After asking a few questions, I learned that he had grown up on a farm, driven a tractor since he was 8 years old, and worked 20 to 40 hours a week—even when going to school full-time. He was never paid for his work but was now a 20-percent owner of the family farm, which was worth more than $500,000. Rather than saying he had never had a job, he learned to speak of his actual experience:

"I'm only 22 years old, but I've worked in my family's business since I was 8 years old. I am used to working hard and getting things done on a deadline. Although I have worked full-time while going to school, my grades are good—particularly in math. I am committed to being a good programmer."

Step 2: Selecting

On both your childhood and adult lists, circle the tasks you did well.

Step 3: Analyzing

Now write all the skills you used to do the task well. Repeat this for each task you circled in Step 2. Use a separate sheet of paper if necessary.

Task 1 skills: _____

_____

_____

Task 2 skills: _____

_____

_____

Task 3 skills: _____

_____

_____

Task 4 skills: _____

_____

_____

Task 5 skills: _____

_____

_____

Step 4: The Final Five

From the skills you listed in Step 3, pick the five you enjoyed using the most and/or did best.

1. _____

2. _____

3. _____

4. _____

5. _____

For some of the significant family responsibilities you identified in Steps 1 and 2, you may also want to complete the Volunteer and Work History exercises later in this chapter. If you were or are a homemaker, this is particularly useful.

Education

The Early Years

For most of us, the early years of schooling were designed to "civilize" us. We learned to read, to count, and to memorize facts. But during that time, we also managed to acquire other basic skills that are important in most jobs:

▼ getting along with others

▼ reading instructions

▼ accepting supervision

How many more can you think of?

While there are dozens of basic skills acquired in early education, try to list only those that relate to your current career interests. Use additional sheets of paper if necessary.

High School

From eighth grade on, courses become more specialized and relevant to potential careers. Complete the following steps to review your high school experience.

Step 1: Remembering

In the following exercise, list the types of courses you took. (If you took three years of English, for example, you don't need to list three courses—just English will do.) For each course, complete the remaining columns:

▼ **Enjoy:** If you enjoyed the course, put a check mark in this column.

▼ **Career:** If you are aware of a direct link between the course and a career or job you are planning to pursue, check this column.

▼ **Support:** Check this column if the course is needed to support success in a career that interests you. For example, if you took business courses and checked the Career column, you might check math as a supportive subject.

41

High School Grid

Course	Enjoy	Career	Support
_____	_____	_____	_____
_____	_____	_____	_____
_____	_____	_____	_____
_____	_____	_____	_____
_____	_____	_____	_____
_____	_____	_____	_____
_____	_____	_____	_____
_____	_____	_____	_____
_____	_____	_____	_____

Step 2: Selecting

Circle the five courses most important to you from Step 1.

Some courses are more important to certain careers than others. But even courses that don't seem to support a particular career choice can be an important source of skills. For example, if you want to be an engineer, doing well in history could demonstrate your memory skills or your attention to detail. That interest could also lead you to consider specializing in the restoration of old buildings or bridges.

You might also choose specific subjects from within a course area. If you are unsure of a specific job objective, select those subjects that interested you or that relate to a career that interests you. If you already have a specific job objective, select those courses that relate to or support your choice.

Step 3: Analyzing

For each of the five courses you selected in Step 2, answer the following questions.

Course 1: _____

What important concepts or skills did you learn? _____

_____

_____

What transferable skills did you use? _____

_____

_____

List any tools, machinery, or equipment you learned to use.

_____

_____

Did you receive any awards or other indicators of doing well?

_____

_____

Course 2: _____

What important concepts or skills did you learn? _____

_____

_____

What transferable skills did you use? _____

_____

_____

List any tools, machinery, or equipment you learned to use.

_____

_____

Did you receive any awards or other indicators of doing well?

_____

Course 3: _____

What important concepts or skills did you learn? _____

_____

_____

_____

What transferable skills did you use? _____

_____

_____

List any tools, machinery, or equipment you learned to use.

_____

_____

Did you receive any awards or other indicators of doing well?

_____

_____

Course 4: _____

What important concepts or skills did you learn? _____

_____

_____

What transferable skills did you use? _____

_____

_____

List any tools, machinery, or equipment you learned to use.

_____

_____

Did you receive any awards or other indicators of doing well?

_____

Course 5: _____

What important concepts or skills did you learn? _____

_____

_____

_____

What transferable skills did you use? _____

_____

_____

List any tools, machinery, or equipment you learned to use.

_____

_____

Did you receive any awards or other indicators of doing well?

_____

_____

Step 4: Reflecting

Do you feel you've had a good basic education? _____

If yes, what did you learn that you do particularly well and that might be useful in
most jobs?

_____

_____

_____

_____

If no, what are the weak areas that have limited or are likely to limit your success
on a job?

_____

_____

_____

_____

Basic skills, such as reading, math, and spoken and written communication are more
important on some jobs than others. If you have a weakness in a basic area and you want
a job in which that might be a problem, consider enrolling in adult basic education
courses or getting special tutoring.

Extracurricular Activities

Participation in sports, clubs, and other extracurricular activities can demonstrate that you are a hard worker or have other valuable skills.

Complete the following exercise to determine your outside interests and activities, which can give you many helpful clues for planning your career.

Job Experience Through Outside Activities

Step 1: Remembering

List all extracurricular activities (include those from your school years) such as music, sports, and clubs.

_____

_____

_____

_____

_____

_____

Step 2: Selecting

If you spent a significant number of hours in an activity, learned or accomplished anything of importance, or were recognized for your achievement or participation, it could be useful in your job search. Circle those activities from your list in Step 1.

Step 3: Analyzing

Answer the following questions for each noteworthy extracurricular activity. Use extra paper if necessary.

Activity 1: _____

What did you do? _____

_____

How many hours per week/month/year did you devote to activity?

_____

What did you learn? _____

_____

What did you accomplish or achieve? _____

_____

_____

What transferable skills did you use? _____

_____

_____

Activity 2: _____

What did you do? _____

_____

How many hours per week/month/year did you devote to activity?

_____

What did you learn? _____

_____

What did you accomplish or achieve? _____

_____

_____

What transferable skills did you use? _____

_____

_____

Activity 3: _____

What did you do? _____

_____

How many hours per week/month/year did you devote to activity?

_____

What did you learn? _____

_____

What did you accomplish or achieve? _____

_____

_____

What transferable skills did you use? _____

_____

_____

Military and Technical Training

Training you receive in a technical or business school can give you an important advantage in the job market. Military training often teaches nonmilitary job-related skills that form the basis for later career success. Technical courses in high school or on-the-job technical training are applicable here as well.

Job Experience Through Special Training

Step 1: Analyzing

For each major source of technical training, answer the following questions. (If you attended several schools or have multiple sources of training, use additional sheets of paper.)

Program or Subject Area: _____

Name or title of specific courses or topics covered: _____

_____

_____

_____

_____

_____

Dates of training: _____

Length of training: Number of hours _____, weeks _____, or years _____.

Class hours per week: _____ Total number of hours in training: _____

Did you receive a certificate of completion, a license, or other proof of competence? If yes, provide details: _____

_____

_____

_____

List five reasons why you chose this school or program of study:

1. _____

2. _____

3. _____

4. _____

5. _____

List ten ways this training has prepared you for your job choice:

1. _____

2. _____

3. _____

4. _____

5. _____

6. _____

7. _____

8. _____

9. _____

10. _____

List three of your most successful or enjoyable experiences involved with this training and provide details.

Successful/Enjoyable Experience 1:

Why? _____

_____

_____

Successful/Enjoyable Experience 2:

Why? _____

_____

_____

Successful/Enjoyable Experience 3:

Why? _____

_____

_____

List every tool, machine, or piece of equipment you used or learned about during your training.

Tools	Machines	Equipment
_____	_____	_____
_____	_____	_____
_____	_____	_____
_____	_____	_____
_____	_____	_____
_____	_____	_____
_____	_____	_____
_____	_____	_____
_____	_____	_____
_____	_____	_____

Conferences, Workshops, and Seminars

Conferences, workshops, and seminars are often sources of highly targeted training.

Highly Targeted Training and Job Skills

Step 1: Remembering

List any such training you have received. As in the earlier exercise on school courses, put check marks in the appropriate columns when

▼ you *enjoyed* the training (Enjoy),

▼ the training is *career-related* (Career),

▼ the training indirectly *supports* your career objective (Support).

Conference, Workshop and Seminar Grid

Event	Enjoy	Career	Support
_____	_____	_____	_____
_____	_____	_____	_____
_____	_____	_____	_____
_____	_____	_____	_____
_____	_____	_____	_____
_____	_____	_____	_____
_____	_____	_____	_____
_____	_____	_____	_____

Step 2: Selecting

Circle those training events that are most important to you. You can evaluate these as you did the training in the previous section. Sometimes a cluster of events—or even a single workshop—can be as important as a more comprehensive, formal course of study.

51

College and Beyond

Employers will be interested in any advanced education you have—whether or not it relates directly to the job you seek. They assume that any education or significant life experience is of possible benefit to them. This assumption is valid, as statistics show that the higher the level of education, the lower the rate of unemployment. On average, people with fewer than four years of high school are unemployed 600 percent more than those with more than four years of college!

Job Skills from Advanced Training

Step 1: Remembering

What majors or subject concentrations did you pursue? ("General studies" could be listed if you did not go far enough to specialize.)

_____   _____

_____   _____

_____   _____

Step 2: Analyzing

For each major or concentration listed in Step 1, answer the following questions. (If you want to analyze more than one subject area, use additional paper as necessary.)

Subject Area 1: _____

Why were you originally interested in this subject area? _____

_____

In general, what skills did you use or learn to use that could be useful in a career?

_____

_____

_____

What did you like most about the subject area? _____

_____

_____

What did you like least about the subject area? _____

_____

_____

What specific courses did you take in the subject area? On a separate sheet of paper, list appropriate courses and provide these details:

▼   Course title

▼   Length (number of weeks/number of hours per week)

▼   Grade

▼   What you liked about this course

If this course directly relates to one of your career objectives, state how. If not, in what way could this course support your career success? (For example, by teaching you good communication skills, problem solving, discipline, analysis, etc.)

Subject Area 2: _____

Why were you originally interested in this subject area? _____

_____

In general, what skills did you use or learn to use that could be useful in a career?

_____

_____

_____

What did you like most about the subject area? _____

_____

_____

What did you like least about the subject area? _____

_____

_____

What specific courses did you take in the subject area? On a separate sheet of paper, list appropriate courses and provide these details:

▼ Course title

▼ Length (number of weeks/number of hours per week)

▼ Grade

▼ What you liked about this course

If this course directly relates to one of your career objectives, state how. If not, in what way could the course support your career success? (For example, did it teach you good communication skills, problem solving, discipline, etc.)

Volunteer and Work History

The primary difference between volunteer work and "regular" work is pay. They are similar in many other aspects, and so are treated in the same way here. Since employers will look closely at your work history, you should complete this section carefully.

If your work experience is limited, you will have to use what you have to your best advantage—including your schooling, training, and other life experiences.

If you have had many jobs, this section will take more time—and work—for you. It is better to be too thorough here than not thorough enough. You may want to skip over some short-term or less important jobs, but even these can be worthwhile to examine as a group. You never know where you may find a spark of insight that could be helpful in a job interview.

Step 1: Remembering

List every job (volunteer and paid) you have ever done. (Use additional paper if needed.)

Organization Name	Your Title	Dates
_____	_____	_____
_____	_____	_____
_____	_____	_____
_____	_____	_____
_____	_____	_____
_____	_____	_____
_____	_____	_____

Step 2: Analyzing

For each job or volunteer position, answer the following questions. Begin with the most recent job, followed by the next most recent and so on. (Use additional paper if necessary.)

Job 1

Name of organization: _____

Address: _____

Phone: _____

Title of position: _____

Employed from: _____ to: _____

Number of hours/week: _____

Salary at start: _____ Final salary: _____

Answer the questions in each section that follows. Look over your responses and decide what parts of the job you liked and disliked. Circle the appropriate answer.

What tools, machines, or equipment did you use?

_____ Like   Dislike

_____ Like   Dislike

_____ Like   Dislike

_____ Like   Dislike

_____ Like   Dislike

_____ Like   Dislike

_____ Like   Dislike

_____ Like   Dislike

_____ Like   Dislike

What types of data, information, or reports did you create or use in the position?

_____ Like   Dislike

_____ Like   Dislike

_____ Like   Dislike

_____   Like   Dislike

_____   Like   Dislike

_____   Like   Dislike

_____   Like   Dislike

_____   Like   Dislike

_____   Like   Dislike

List any duties or responsibilities that were people-oriented (involved co-workers, superiors, employees, customers).

_____   Like   Dislike

_____   Like   Dislike

_____   Like   Dislike

_____   Like   Dislike

_____   Like   Dislike

_____   Like   Dislike

_____   Like   Dislike

_____   Like   Dislike

_____   Like   Dislike

What other duties and responsibilities did you have? (Be specific.)

_____   Like   Dislike

_____   Like   Dislike

_____   Like   Dislike

_____   Like   Dislike

_____   Like   Dislike

_____   Like   Dislike

_____   Like   Dislike

_____   Like   Dislike

_____   Like   Dislike

What services did you provide or what products did you produce?

_____	Like	Dislike
_____	Like	Dislike
_____	Like	Dislike
_____	Like	Dislike
_____	Like	Dislike
_____	Like	Dislike
_____	Like	Dislike
_____	Like	Dislike
_____	Like	Dislike
_____	Like	Dislike

Did you ever train, _____ supervise, _____ or instruct _____ anyone on this job?

To do what? _____

_____

_____

Did you receive any promotions or salary increases for your performance?
If yes, provide details:

_____

_____

_____

Provide details of anything you did to help the company, such as increase productivity, simplify or reorganize job duties, decrease costs, increase profits, improve working conditions, or reduce turnover. Qualify results where possible: for example, "Increased order processing by 50 percent, with no increase in staff costs."

_____

_____

_____

What did you learn on this job?

_____

_____

_____

_____

What did you like most about this job?

_____

_____

_____

_____

_____

What did you like least?

_____

_____

_____

_____

_____

Why did you leave? (Or why are you still there?)

_____

_____

_____

_____

What would your supervisor say about you?

_____

_____

_____

_____

Job 2

Name of organization: _____

Address: _____

Phone: _____

Title of position: _____

Employed from: _____ to: _____

   Number of hours/week: _____

   Salary at start: _____ Final salary: _____

Answer the questions in each section that follows. Look over your responses and decide what parts of the job you liked and disliked. Circle the appropriate answer.

What tools, machines, or equipment did you use?

_____	Like	Dislike
_____	Like	Dislike
_____	Like	Dislike
_____	Like	Dislike
_____	Like	Dislike
_____	Like	Dislike
_____	Like	Dislike
_____	Like	Dislike
_____	Like	Dislike
_____	Like	Dislike

What types of data, information, or reports did you create or use in the position?

_____	Like	Dislike
_____	Like	Dislike
_____	Like	Dislike
_____	Like	Dislike
_____	Like	Dislike

_____   Like   Dislike

_____   Like   Dislike

_____   Like   Dislike

_____   Like   Dislike

_____   Like   Dislike

List any duties or responsibilities that were people-oriented (involved co-workers, superiors, employees, customers).

_____   Like   Dislike

_____   Like   Dislike

_____   Like   Dislike

_____   Like   Dislike

_____   Like   Dislike

_____   Like   Dislike

_____   Like   Dislike

_____   Like   Dislike

_____   Like   Dislike

_____   Like   Dislike

What other duties and responsibilities did you have? (Be specific.)

_____   Like   Dislike

_____   Like   Dislike

_____   Like   Dislike

_____   Like   Dislike

_____   Like   Dislike

_____   Like   Dislike

_____   Like   Dislike

_____   Like   Dislike

_____   Like   Dislike

_____   Like   Dislike

What services did you provide or what products did you produce?

_____	Like	Dislike
_____	Like	Dislike
_____	Like	Dislike
_____	Like	Dislike
_____	Like	Dislike
_____	Like	Dislike
_____	Like	Dislike
_____	Like	Dislike
_____	Like	Dislike
_____	Like	Dislike

Did you ever train, _____ supervise, _____ or instruct _____ anyone on this job?

To do what? _____

_____

_____

Did you receive any promotions or salary increases for your performance? If yes, provide details:

_____

_____

Provide details of anything you did to help the company, such as increase productivity, simplify or reorganize job duties, decrease costs, increase profits, improve working conditions, or reduce turnover. Qualify results where possible: for example, "Increased order processing by 50 percent, with no increase in staff costs."

_____

_____

_____

_____

_____

What did you learn on this job?

_____

_____

_____

_____

What did you like most about this job?

_____

_____

_____

_____

What did you like least?

_____

_____

_____

_____

Why did you leave? (Or why are you still there?)

_____

_____

_____

_____

What would your supervisor say about you?

_____

_____

_____

_____

Define the Ideal Job for You

As kids, when we thought about work, most of us could name a specific interest. "I want to be a teacher," we would say. Or, "I want to be a firefighter." But that was play. Few of us get serious about career decisions until we are of working age, and even then, few of us actually settle on careers until we're in our late 20s or early 30s.

The current edition of the *Dictionary of Occupational Titles* lists more than 20,000 job titles. While that number seems staggering, remember that each and every job is as unique as the person who fills it. Seriously considering all 20,000 job titles is out of the question, of course, so our task is to narrow your field down to the type of jobs you want. Developing a *job objective* accomplishes this and helps you take the next step: targeting a specific job.

If You Don't Know What You Want to Do

If you have not yet arrived at a specific career decision, a job objective will help you establish a direction. Without a job objective—specific or general—you will have a hard time telling most employers why they should hire you. "Needing the money" is definitely *not* a good argument, and you could hardly tell them you are "just right for the job"— whatever it is. You are at a distinct disadvantage compared to a job seeker who wants *that* job and can give good reasons why he or she can handle it.

It is perfectly okay to change your job objective during your job search, but it is not wise to say you are willing to take "anything." The more specific you can be about what you want, the more likely you are to find what you're looking for. If you go out looking for "anything," your job search will become a haphazard blind man's bluff—lots of confusion and no telling where you'll end up.

If You *Do* Know What You Want to Do

If you know what job you want, you might think you have a sufficiently defined job objective, and you might be tempted to skip this section. Resist the temptation. You'll fare better on your job search if you follow through on these exercises. They will give you a focus that makes your search for suitable work more efficient. Also, as you learn to communicate what you want with confidence and precision, you'll gain a competitive edge over less-prepared job applicants.

What Do You Want from Work?

Reading through this list of work characteristics will help you understand the many issues involved in making a career decision.

Checklist of Work Characteristics[1]

Begin by reading through the entire list to understand each of the issues listed. Then go over the list again. This time, consider how important each is to you. Use the following scale to rate each item.

1 = Not important at all   *2 = Not very important*
3 = Somewhat important   *4 = Very important*

_____ **Help society:** Contribute to the betterment of the world

_____ **Help others:** Help other people directly, either individually or in small groups

_____ **Public contact:** Have lots of day-to-day contact with people

_____ **Work with others:** Have a close working relationship with a group; work as a team member toward common goals

_____ **Affiliation:** Be a member of an organization whose work or status is important to me

_____ **Friendship:** Develop close, personal relationships with co-workers

_____ **Competition:** Pit my abilities against others in events for which there are clear outcomes

_____ **Make decisions:** Have the power to set policy and determine a course of action

_____ **Work under pressure:** Work in a situation in which deadlines and high-quality work are required

_____ **Power and authority:** Control other people's work activities

_____ **Influence people:** Be in a position to change others' attitudes and opinions

_____ **Work alone:** Do things by myself, without much contact with others

_____ **Knowledge:** Seek knowledge, truth, and understanding

_____ **Intellectual status:** Be regarded as a person of intellectual achievement or as an expert

_____ **Artistic creativity:** Do creative work in any of several art forms

_____ **Creativity:** Create new ideas, programs, organizational structures, or anything else that has not been developed by others

_____ **Aesthetics:** Have a job that involves sensitivity to beauty

_____ **Supervise:** Guide other people in their work

_____ **Change and variety:** Have job duties that often change or that are done in different settings

_____ **Precision work:** Do work with little margin for error

_____ **Stability:** Have job duties that are largely predictable and are not likely to change over a long period of time

_____ **Security:** Be assured of keeping my job and receiving reasonable financial reward

_____ **Fast pace:** Work quickly, keep up with a fast pacc

_____ **Recognition:** Be recognized for the quality of my work in some visible or public way

_____ **Excitement:** Do work that is very exciting or that often is exciting

_____ **Adventure:** Do work that requires me to take risks

_____ **Profit, gain:** Expect to earn large amounts of money or gain other material possessions

_____ **Independence:** Decide for myself what kind of work I'll do and how I'll go about it; not have to obey others

_____ **Moral fulfillment:** Feel that my work is contributing to a set of moral standards that are important to me

_____ **Location:** Find a place to live (town, geographic area) that matches my lifestyle and allows me to do the things I enjoy

_____ **Community:** Live in a town or city where I can get involved in community affairs

_____ **Physical challenge:** Have a job whose physical demands are challenging and rewarding

_____ **Time freedom:** Handle my job according to my own time schedule, with no specific working hours required

Your Ideal Work Characteristics

Now, in the space below, write the work characteristics that are most important to you (the characteristics that you rated as 4s). This is *your* list, so be sure to include anything else important to you in your work, even if it was not included in the list.

_____   _____

_____   _____

_____   _____

_____   _____

_____   _____

_____   _____

_____   _____

_____   _____

_____   _____

Define the Ideal Job

Your ideal job would include many of the general work characteristics in the preceding list, but there are ways to develop a more specific job objective that's right for you. Virtually every job description can be broken down into a few simple elements.

 skills

 personal values

▼ earnings

▼ level of responsibility

▼ location

▼ special knowledge

▼ work environment

▼ types of people

All of these elements interact in any job, so before you define your ideal job, you should explore each of these factors in more detail.

Skills

Earlier you developed a list of skills and specific situations in which you have used them. Having a good knowledge of your key skills is essential in developing a job objective.

Go back to Chapter 2 and find your lists of top five adaptive skills and top five transferable skills. Write them below:

Top Five Adaptive Skills	Top Five Transferable Skills
1. _____	1. _____
2. _____	2. _____
3. _____	3. _____
4. _____	4. _____
5. _____	5. _____

Personal Values

Some of the items on the Checklist of Work Characteristics relate to your values (or what motivates you). Do you want to help others? To make lots of money? To gain power or recognition? There are usually several values that motivate us, but we often overlook them when making career choices. The following "Uncle Mort" exercises can help you identify your values.

Poor Old Uncle Mort

Imagine getting a telegram informing you of the death of a distant and unknown relative, Uncle Mort. Well, poor old Uncle Mort, it turns out, had lots of money. He's left you $10 million. That's right, *ten million dollars!* Before you go out and celebrate, though, there are a few things Uncle Mort wanted you to do (before you get the money).

First, Uncle Mort wanted you to take a year to learn something—anything—you were interested in. You'll get $50,000 during this time. Write what you want to learn.

_____

_____

_____

_____

_____

_____

_____

_____

Living on Easy Street

Okay, you've spent your year learning something; now you get the rest of the $10 million. You don't have to work, so how will you spend your time now: where, with whom, doing what? Think about this. What will you be doing in five years? In ten?

Now (include what, where, with whom): _____

_____

_____

_____

In five years: _____

_____

_____

_____

In ten years: _____

_____

_____

_____

Taking Stock of Your Accomplishments

Now that you've had a good time, let's get more serious. Imagine your 90th birthday party. Someone there gives a speech reviewing the things you've accomplished during your lifetime. What would you like that person to say about you?

_____

_____

_____

_____

_____

If You Could Change the World

You are about to join Uncle Mort in "millionaires' heaven." During your lifetime, what sort of world problems would you like to have seen solved? Write those that are particularly meaningful to you.

_____

_____

_____

_____

_____

_____

These simple exercises give you hints of the things that are really important to you. Of course, there are all kinds of practical barriers and personal responsibilities that prevent us from doing many of these things. The truth is that we have to make choices, and many of these choices involve compromises. But you have far more ability to define your future than you might think. If you really want to sail around the world, write a novel, or live in the mountains, the task is to define the short-term goals you can reach *now* to get you closer to the long-term ones.

Earnings

A classic interview question is, "How much money are you looking for?" I have always been tempted to answer, "How much have you lost?" If you don't know what to say, you will probably lose.

It always surprises me how little thought most people give to how much money they want or expect to make. For example, I once asked an inexperienced young man how much he expected to earn on his next job. He answered, "About $40,000." He had never worked full-time for longer than two months and had never earned more than $4.50 per hour! Just as unprepared are those who say they will work for "anything."

Case Study: Charlie

I remember a middle-aged executive who had made more than $70,000 per year. Then he lost his job and was unemployed for over a year. When I asked what he wanted to earn in his next job, he told me that he *wanted* to start at about $75,000, but that he really only *needed* $40,000 per year to maintain his lifestyle since his children were grown. I suggested that he redefine his job objectives to find something that interested him, and that he not screen out jobs paying less than $70,000 per year. Eventually he took a job paying $41,000, and he loved it. He told me he would never even consider going back to what he had done before—whatever the salary.

What Do You Expect to Earn?

Directions: Complete the following questions to help you define a salary range. (All figures should be for gross salary—before taxes are withheld.)

1. *Ideally*, what would you like to earn to maintain the lifestyle you want? _____

   _____

2. What kind of weekly or annual salary do you need to pay for a *modest* lifestyle? (To determine this, you have to figure out what that lifestyle costs. If you're not sure, a librarian can help you find information on average expenses.) Write the figures below, based on a full-time job.

   Per Week _____   Per Year _____

3. If you found the perfect job in all other respects, what is the very *lowest* salary you would accept? _____

   Your salary ranges are:

   a. Ideal (from question 1): _____

   b. Desirable (from question 2): _____

   c. Minimum (from question 3): _____

Level of Responsibility

If you want to earn lots of money but don't want to have lots of responsibility, you are in for a rude awakening. Most jobs that pay well have more responsibility than those paying less. Of course, there are exceptions—such as being a rock star—but the competition for those jobs is fierce, and there is often more responsibility required than meets the eye.

A general rule is this: The higher up you are in an organization, the more you make.

1. Do you like to be in charge of things? _____

2. Are you good at supervising others? _____

3. Do you prefer working as part of a group? _____

4. Do you prefer to work by yourself under someone else's guidance? _____

5. Do you like working by yourself but independently?_____

There are no right or wrong answers to these questions, but once you have answered them, go back and review your salary expectations. If you answered yes to number 4 and you want to make a lot of money, you might have a problem.

Location

Are you willing to relocate? This is an important question to answer now—before it comes up in an interview. There often are good reasons for wanting to stay where you are, but certain jobs and career opportunities are limited unless you are willing to move. If you want to live in Kansas, for example, but you want to be an undersea cable technician, job opportunities will be limited, to say the least. You will have to change your job objective or relocate.

If you live in a rural area or small town, certain jobs are limited and the pay scale is often lower. You may have to compromise on your job objective, relocate, or go without employment. For example, plumbing jobs are not particularly rare, but if there are only three plumbing contractors in a 50-mile radius of where you live, job opportunities in that field will be limited. You may have to move to a larger population center or consider another line of work.

If you feel sure you want to live where you are now, do the following exercise before locking yourself into the decision. It will help you determine whether the compromises involved in relocating might be worthwhile.

To Stay or Not to Stay

Write the pros and cons of relocating in the spaces below. Be sure to discuss this with others, especially those who will be affected by your decision.

Advantages of Staying

For Me	For Others
_____	_____
_____	_____
_____	_____
_____	_____
_____	_____
_____	_____

Advantages of Leaving

<table>
<tr><td>For Me</td><td>For Others</td></tr>
<tr><td>_____</td><td>_____</td></tr>
<tr><td>_____</td><td>_____</td></tr>
<tr><td>_____</td><td>_____</td></tr>
<tr><td>_____</td><td>_____</td></tr>
<tr><td>_____</td><td>_____</td></tr>
<tr><td>_____</td><td>_____</td></tr>
</table>

Key Idea

Remember, the narrower your job search is, the easier it is to do it well.

When you have looked at all the angles, you can make an informed decision. If you *prefer* to stay but are *willing* to move, a good strategy is to spend most of your time searching for a local job.

Do what you can to limit the geographic area of your search. The longer you remain unemployed, however, the more time you should spend looking elsewhere.

Consider your access to transportation and how far you are willing to commute. If you use public transportation, you must limit your job search to places within walking distance of the routes. Consider whether you prefer to work on the north, south, east, or west side of town.

Tips for Deciding Whether to Relocate

Here are a few more points to consider when you are thinking about relocating:

▼ If you live in a rural area, do not have a vehicle, and do not have access to public transportation, find someone who commutes regularly. Ask that person for a ride, and concentrate your job search along his or her route. (Do offer to pay expenses once you begin working!)

▼ If you are willing to relocate, don't make the mistake of looking for a job just anywhere. That sort of scattered approach is not efficient or effective. I have counseled many people who have relocated out of desperation or before studying the consequences. The resulting personal and financial problems can be devastating. Many lost their homes and possessions in the process. It is rarely a good idea to move first and look for work later!

▼ Narrow your job search to a few key geographic areas and concentrate your efforts there. One strategy is to identify where the best job opportunities are for the sort of job you want. (A librarian can help you find this information.) But this should not be the only thing you think about. Every year, countless people take a job "somewhere" only to find that (a) they hate the place, (b) they can't afford to live there, or (c) there is no indoor plumbing. The right job in the wrong place is not the right job.

▼ Define the characteristics of the place you'd like to live. For example, suppose you want to live near the ocean, in a fairly large but not overly crowded city, and in a part of the country that has four seasons but mild winters. That leaves out New York and Miami (and lots of other places, too), doesn't it? As you add criteria, there are fewer and fewer places to consider, and your job search becomes more precise. Do the following exercise if you are considering relocating.

Determining Geographic Preference

To complete the following exercise, think about all the places you have lived or visited. Since it is often easier to define dislikes, start by listing the things you did *not* like about these places. Once you have done that, redefine these negatives into positives. (For example, "I hated the smog in L.A." becomes "I want to live in a place with clean air.")

When your list is complete, circle the five or ten location factors that are most important to you. Use this list to select a few key areas in which to concentrate your job search. If you haven't done much traveling, there are a couple of interesting books that might help you. *Best Towns in America* (by Bayless) reviews 50 of the most desirable locations in the U.S. *Greener Pastures Relocation Guide* evaluates the various states by what they have to offer. Again, the library is a good place to get details on various locations.

Place: _____

Things I Did Not Like	**Things I Would Like**
_____	_____
_____	_____
_____	_____
_____	_____
_____	_____

Place: _____

Things I Did Not Like	**Things I Would Like**
_____	_____
_____	_____
_____	_____
_____	_____

Place: _____

Things I Did Not Like	Things I Would Like
_____	_____
_____	_____
_____	_____
_____	_____
_____	_____

Place: _____

Things I Did Not Like	Things I Would Like
_____	_____
_____	_____
_____	_____
_____	_____
_____	_____

Place: _____

Things I Did Not Like	Things I Would Like
_____	_____
_____	_____
_____	_____
_____	_____
_____	_____

Special Knowledge

In addition to your training and education, you may also have special knowledge gained from a hobby, volunteer activity, a previous job, or other sources. Such knowledge is another factor to consider when developing a job objective. Refer back to the work you did in Chapter 3. Reviewing the detailed analysis of your history will make it easy to identify the things you know particularly well. The following exercise helps you identify your areas of expertise that might be used in your "ideal" job.

List below the major areas in which you

▼ have knowledge and experience,

▼ have received formal education or training,

▼ are very interested, but don't have much practical experience.

_____

_____

_____

_____

_____

_____

_____

_____

_____

Once you've made your list, select the three areas that are most interesting to you.

If you already have a job objective that does not use any of your top three areas of special knowledge, don't toss it out just yet; a combination may be possible. For instance, if you are looking for a job as a supermarket warehouse manager, but you selected your hobby of making pottery as one of the three, can you think of a job combining the two? Perhaps you could work for a pottery distributor or manage some part of a pottery business.

Work Environment

I don't like to work in a building without windows, and I like to be able to get up and move around occasionally. While most of us can put up with all kinds of less-than-ideal aspects in a work environment, some factors are more important than others.

Think of all the places you've worked or gone to school (don't forget military training and service). List the aspects you didn't like about those work environments, and then redefine them into positives, as you did with your geographic preferences. When you have completed the list for each job you've had, circle the three environmental preferences that are most important to you.

Job: _____

Things I Did Not Like About the Work Environment	Work Environment I Would Like in My Next Job
_____	_____
_____	_____
_____	_____
_____	_____
_____	_____

Job: _____

Things I Did Not Like About the Work Environment	Work Environment I Would Like in My Next Job
_____	_____
_____	_____
_____	_____
_____	_____
_____	_____

Job: _____

Things I Did Not Like About the Work Environment	Work Environment I Would Like in My Next Job
_____	_____
_____	_____
_____	_____
_____	_____

Job: _____

Things I Did Not Like About the Work Environment	Work Environment I Would Like in My Next Job
_____	_____
_____	_____
_____	_____
_____	_____

Job: _____

Things I Did Not Like About the Work Environment	Work Environment I Would Like in My Next Job
_____	_____
_____	_____
_____	_____
_____	_____

Types of People

After salary, the next job element listed as important by most workers is the type of people they work with. If you've ever had a rotten boss or worked with a group you didn't like, you know exactly why this is so important. But someone else's definition of a good group of co-workers might not be your definition. You might argue that you can't know in advance who will your co-workers will be, but if you haven't given it any thought, you can only trust to luck.

Think about all your past jobs (work, military, volunteering, etc.) and your co-workers on those jobs. List the characteristics you didn't like about your co-workers, then redefine them into qualities you'd like to see in your future workmates. When your list is complete, identify the types of people you would really like to work with in your next job. Circle the three qualities that are most important to you.

Job/Co-Workers: _____

Things I Did Not Like About My Co-Workers	Types of People I Would Like to Work with on My Next Job
_____	_____
_____	_____
_____	_____
_____	_____
_____	_____

Job/Co-Workers: _____

Things I Did Not Like About My Co-Workers	Types of People I Would Like to Work with on My Next Job
_____	_____
_____	_____
_____	_____
_____	_____
_____	_____

Job/Co-Workers: _____

Things I Did Not Like About My Co-Workers	Types of People I Would Like to Work with on My Next Job
_____	_____
_____	_____
_____	_____
_____	_____
_____	_____

Job/Co-Workers: _____

<table>
<tr><td>Things I Did Not Like
About My Co-Workers</td><td>Types of People I Would Like
to Work with on My Next Job</td></tr>
</table>

_____   _____

_____   _____

_____   _____

_____   _____

_____   _____

Job/Co-Workers: _____

<table>
<tr><td>Things I Did Not Like
About My Co-Workers</td><td>Types of People I Would Like
to Work with on My Next Job</td></tr>
</table>

_____   _____

_____   _____

_____   _____

_____   _____

_____   _____

Put It All Together

We have explored so many factors involved in defining your ideal job, it may be hard to make sense of it all. One way to sort through your information is to put it down in an organized way. Look at The Job Wheel on the following page.[2] It will help you remember what's important and bring together the details of your choices into one understandable picture.

Using The Job Wheel

The Job Wheel includes each of the factors involved in defining your ideal job. In each section of the wheel, there is space for your top choices from each of the exercises you completed in this chapter. Go back over each exercise now and think about whether you have overlooked anything important. Feel free to add anything you left out before. When you are ready, list your top choices in the appropriate places in each section of The Job Wheel.

Your Job Wheel is unique, just as you are. Your task is to use your Job Wheel to define and find a job that comes as close as possible to meeting the criteria you have selected. If you conduct a creative job search, you won't just be looking for *a* job; you will be looking for *the* job. You will be one of the best-prepared people for that job—even if you don't know just what it is called yet or where it exists.

The Job Wheel does not give you a job title, but it does give you a variety of places to start your job search. For example, let's look at a wheel that was done by a participant in a workshop I led several years ago.

Pam's Job Wheel

Remember Pam from Chapter 2? She was the one competing with 60 other applicants for a position as an advertising copywriter. Before she did her Job Wheel, Pam had great difficulty defining her job objective. I asked the other members of her group to list some jobs she might consider; these were some of the suggestions:

▼ write a corporate newsletter

▼ work for a newspaper

▼ promote special events

▼ help in a political campaign

▼ get into advertising

▼ public relations for nonprofit groups

▼ work for a publishing company

▼ be a freelance editor or graphic designer

▼ work as a secretary for a fine arts organization

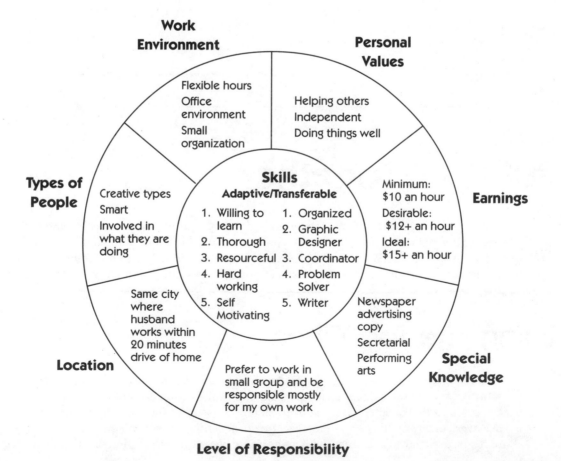

80

There were other suggestions too, and perhaps you could think of more. The point is that The Job Wheel provides ideas of what to look for in a job, as well as ideas of where to look. Pam did follow up on her wheel. She now works for a museum, promoting special events, writing a regular newsletter to museum patrons, and directing the museum's public relations.

Your Job Wheel

Now it's time to create your own Job Wheel by writing your own criteria in the wheel on the following page. When you combine the various elements of your wheel in new ways, many job possibilities will present themselves.

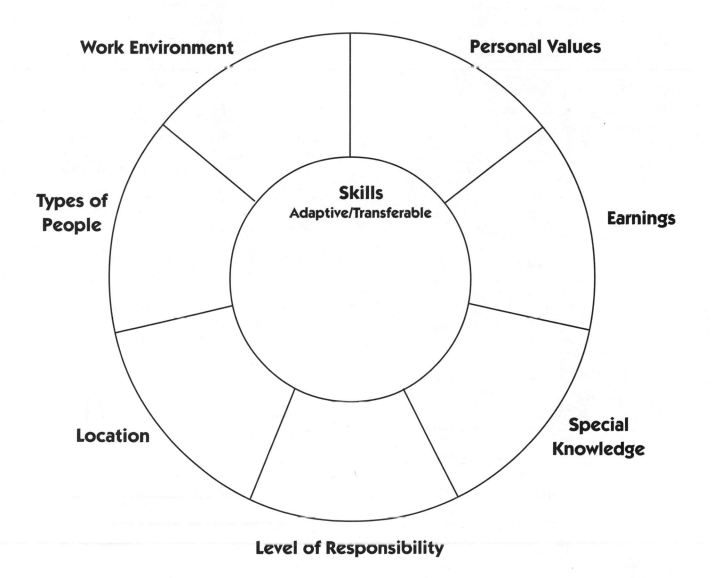

Work Environment

Personal Values

Skills
Adaptive/Transferable

Earnings

Types of People

Special Knowledge

Location

Level of Responsibility

Case Study: Larry

After leaving the army, Larry earned a two-year associate degree in law enforcement, but he could not find a job in that field. He enrolled in a travel school and was to graduate during one of the worst recessions in the travel industry; a job in that field seemed unlikely as well. He was discouraged and felt he had no hope of finding a good job. We did the grid in his workshop group, and the travel/law enforcement combination came up. Someone suggested he look into security at an airport—an idea that had never occurred to him. He contacted the airport and spoke with the head of security. She said she had never met someone with experience in law enforcement and special training in the travel industry, but that she had no openings at that time.

However, she called Larry back within a few days and offered him a job she had created for him—as a supervisor on the second shift.

The Jobs Grid

One way to create new ideas for job possibilities is to combine elements from your Job Wheel and from other sources and then organize them in a grid. Look at the example below, which was filled out by a job seeker.

Where the columns meet, there are boxes in which combinations can be considered for potential job ideas. In the example, the left column contains all the things this job seeker knew a lot about (from training, school, work experience, military, hobbies, and other sources). Along the top, the person wrote the things he or she was really interested in and could do well (skills). Where each column meets, he or she wrote 1 if the combination sounded very interesting, 2 if it sounded somewhat interesting, and 3 if it was not at all interesting. This person marked an X in any box that did not create a combination that made sense.

Sample Jobs Grid

Notice that one of the squares marked 1 is where travel and law enforcement meet. This was exactly the situation with a young man I met several years ago. Read the case study to visualize his jobs grid.

Your Own Jobs Grid

Fill in the blank grid opposite. Where each column meets, rate the combination 1 if it sounds very interesting, 2 if it sounds somewhat interesting, or 3 if it is not interesting at all. Pay close attention to the combinations you mark with a 1. You will be instructed to do some brainstorming on possible jobs and places to work using the combinations that interest you the most.

Sample Jobs Grid

Things You Know About	Law enforcement	Auto racing	Baseball	Organized	Good communication skills	Analyzing
Travel (went to Travel School)	1	1	3	2	3	2
Law inforcement (M.P. in service)	x	2	2	3	3	2
Cars (hobby)	2	2	x	2	3	2
Sports (played in high school)	2	2	3	2	2	2
Farming (grew up on one)	2	x	x	3	3	2

Skills and Interests

Your Own Jobs Grid

Skills and Interests

Things You Know About

Exploring Job Possibilities

In the spaces below, jot down each combination that interests you. Then list as many jobs or places to work as you can think of for each. Don't worry if some of the combinations or ideas don't seem practical; you can work on that later.

Interesting Combinations	Possible Jobs or Places to Work
_____	_____
_____	_____
_____	_____
_____	_____
_____	_____
_____	_____
_____	_____
_____	_____

Even jobs with the same title can be very different from one organization to another. What's important is that you know enough about yourself and about the various elements of a job to evaluate the *fit*. Knowing how to do this is more important to your career satisfaction and success than the selection of a particular job title.

Remember, you might change careers several times, and you probably will change jobs even more often during your working life. You might be faced with the task of defining job and career objectives several times. The self-understanding skills you have learned in this chapter should help you make these transitions with minimum hassle and maximum success.

Chapter 4

1. This exercise comes from Bulletin #2001, "Exploring Careers" (U.S. Department of Labor).

2. The concepts behind the Job Wheel are based on those developed by the late John Crystal and popularized by Richard Bolles. Crystal and Bolles authored *Where Do I Go from Here with the Rest of My Life?* Bolles also authored the best-selling *What Color Is Your Parachute?*

Exploring Career and Job Alternatives

This chapter has two major sections. In the first, we will review major labor market trends. These trends include information you should consider in making your career decision. The second section includes the Job Matching Chart, which provides information on more than 200 major jobs. You can use it to help you identify groups of jobs—and specific jobs—that interest you.

Important Labor Market Trends to Consider in Your Career Planning[1]

In order to make informed career decisions, you need reliable information about opportunities that should be available in the future. This section presents highlights from Bureau of Labor Statistics projections of industry and occupational employment. This information can help guide your career plans.

A slowdown in employment growth is expected.

Between now and the year 2005, our labor market is projected to add 17 million new jobs. This is an increase of 14 percent.

▼ Hourly and salary workers will account for 95 percent of the new jobs, but self-employed workers also are expected to increase by 950,000, to 11.6 million people in 2005.

Service-producing industries will account for most new jobs (see Chart 1).

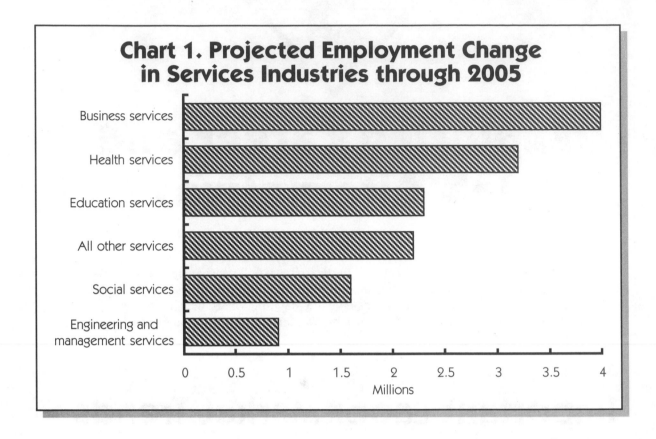

Chart 1. Projected Employment Change in Services Industries through 2005

▼ Employment growth is projected to be highly concentrated by industry. The services and retail trade industries will account for 16.2 million of the projected growth of 16.8 million wage and salary jobs.

▼ Business, health, and educational services will account for 70 percent of the growth—9.2 million of 13.6 million jobs—within services.

▼ Health care services will account for almost one-fifth of all job growth through 2005. The aging population and the increased use of medical technology are factors in this increase. Patients will increasingly be shifted out of hospitals and into outpatient facilities, nursing homes, and home health care in an attempt to contain costs.

▼ The personnel supply services industry, which provides temporary help to employers in other industries, is projected to add 1.3 million jobs by 2005.

The goods-producing sector will decline (see Chart 2).

▼ The goods-producing sector faces declining employment in two of its four industries: manufacturing and mining. Employment in the other two industries—construction and agriculture, forestry, and fishing—is expected to increase.

▼ Employment in manufacturing is expected to continue its decline, losing 1.3 million jobs through 2005. Operators, fabricators, and laborers and precision production, craft, and repair occupations are expected to account for more than 1 million of these lost jobs. Systems analysts and other computer-related occupations in manufacturing are expected to increase.

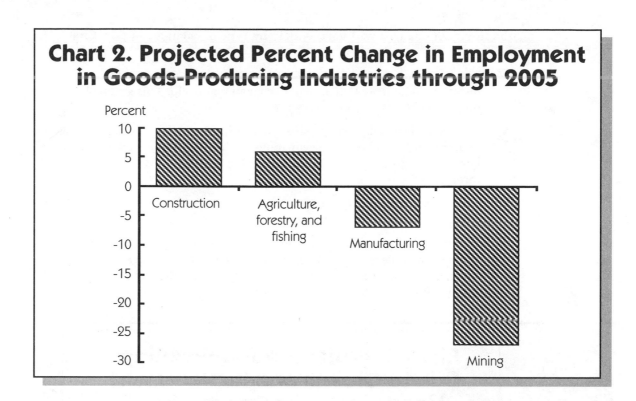

Chart 2. Projected Percent Change in Employment in Goods-Producing Industries through 2005

Job opportunities arise in two ways: job growth and replacement needs (see Chart 3).

▼ Job growth can be measured by percentage changes and numerical changes. The fastest-growing occupations do not necessarily provide the largest numbers of jobs. An occupation that is growing rapidly may provide fewer openings than a slower-growing but larger occupation.

▼ Opportunities in large occupations are created by the need to replace workers who leave these jobs. Some workers leave as they are promoted or change careers; others stop working to return to school, to assume household responsibilities, or to retire.

▼ Replacement needs are greater in occupations with low pay and status, low training requirements, and a high percentage of young and part-time workers.

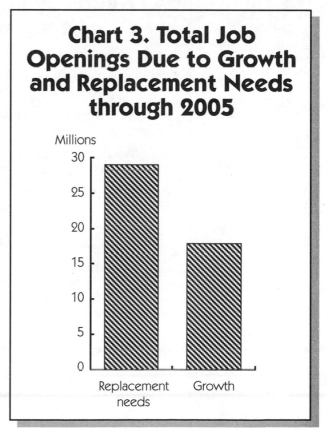

Chart 3. Total Job Openings Due to Growth and Replacement Needs through 2005

▼ Replacement needs will account for 29.4 million job openings by 2005, far more than the 17.7 million openings projected to arise from employment growth.

87

Employment changes will vary widely by type of occupation (see Chart 4).

▼ Employment in professional specialty occupations is projected to increase at a faster rate than in any other major occupational group. This group of jobs also is projected to create the most new jobs.

▼ Professional specialty occupations—which require high educational levels and offer high earnings—and service occupations—which require less education and offer lower earnings—are expected to account for more than half of all job growth through 2005.

▼ Office automation is expected to have a significant effect on many administrative and clerical support occupations.

▼ Precision production, craft, and repair occupations and operators, fabricators, and laborers are projected to grow much more slowly than average due to continuing advances in technology, changes in production methods, and the overall decline in manufacturing employment.

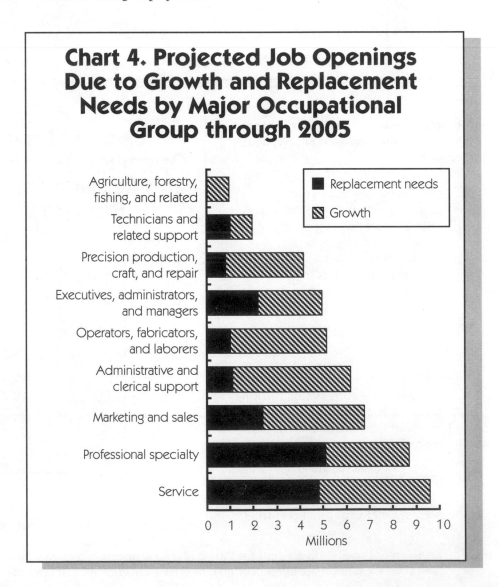

Chart 4. Projected Job Openings Due to Growth and Replacement Needs by Major Occupational Group through 2005

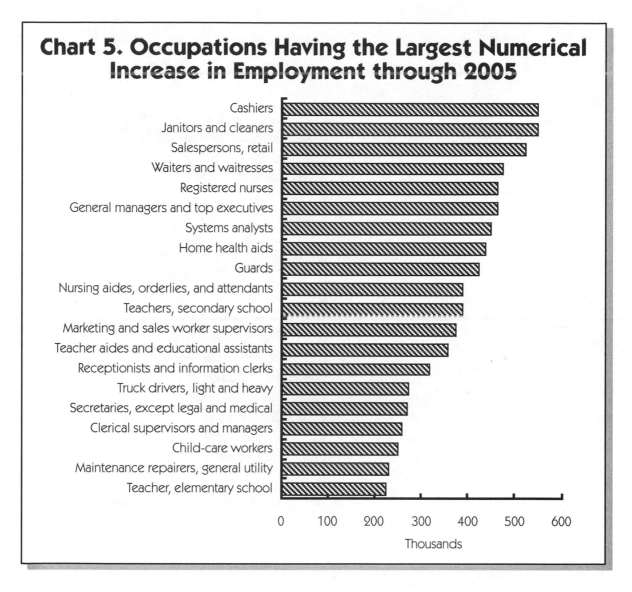

Chart 5. Occupations Having the Largest Numerical Increase in Employment through 2005

Twenty occupations will account for half of all job growth through 2005 (see Chart 5).

▼ The 20 occupations accounting for half of all job growth tend to be large in size rather than fast growing. Three health care occupations are in the top 10, and three education-related occupations are in the second 10.

The fastest-growing occupations reflect growth in computer technology and health services (see Chart 6).

▼ Many of the fastest-growing occupations are concentrated in health services, which are expected to increase more than twice as fast as the economy as a whole. Personal and home care aides and home health aides are expected to be in great demand to provide personal and physical care for an increasing number of elderly people and for persons who are recovering from surgery and other serious health conditions. This is occurring as hospitals and insurance companies mandate shorter stays for recovery to contain costs.

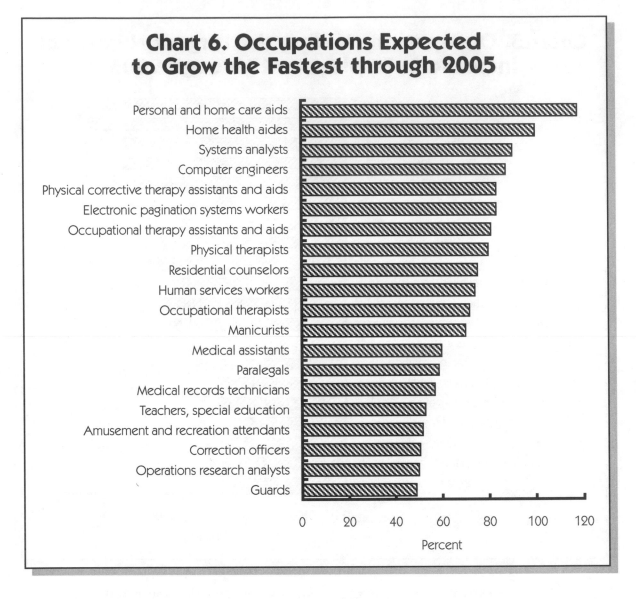

Chart 6. Occupations Expected to Grow the Fastest through 2005

Personal and home care aids
Home health aides
Systems analysts
Computer engineers
Physical corrective therapy assistants and aids
Electronic pagination systems workers
Occupational therapy assistants and aids
Physical therapists
Residential counselors
Human services workers
Occupational therapists
Manicurists
Medical assistants
Paralegals
Medical records technicians
Teachers, special education
Amusement and recreation attendants
Correction officers
Operations research analysts
Guards

0   20   40   60   80   100   120

Percent

▼ Employment of computer engineers and systems analysts is expected to grow rapidly to satisfy expanding needs for scientific research and applications of computer technology in business and industry.

Declining occupational employment stems from declining industry employment and technological change (see Chart 7).

▼ Farmers, garment-sewing machine operators, and private household cleaners and servants are examples of occupations that will lose employment because of declining industry employment.

▼ Many declining occupations are affected by changes resulting from technological advances, organizational changes, and other factors that affect the employment of workers. For example, the use of typists and word processors is expected to decline substantially because of productivity improvements resulting from office automation and the increased use of word processing equipment by professional and managerial employees.

Education and training affect job opportunities (see Chart 8 and Table 1).

▼ Workers in jobs with low education and training requirements tend to change jobs more often. As a result, these jobs will provide a larger than proportional share of all job openings stemming from replacement needs.

▼ Jobs requiring the most education and training will grow faster than jobs with lower education and training requirements.

Table 1 presents the fastest-growing occupations and those having the largest numerical increase in employment, arranged by level of education and training.

Jobs requiring the most education and training will be the fastest growing and highest paying.

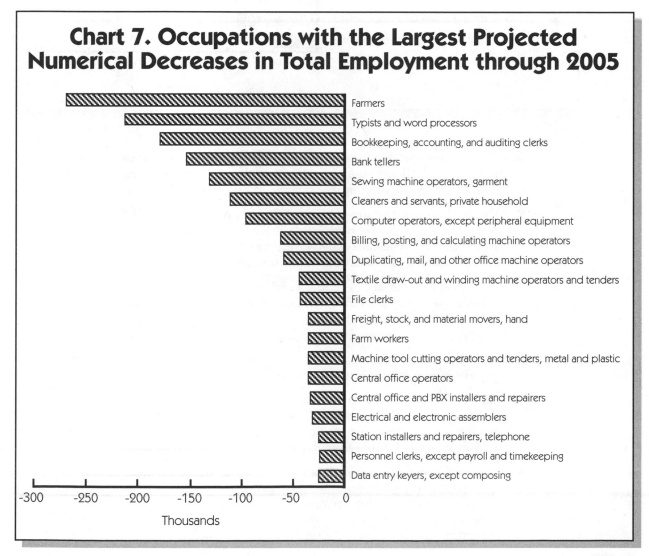

Chart 7. Occupations with the Largest Projected Numerical Decreases in Total Employment through 2005

Farmers
Typists and word processors
Bookkeeping, accounting, and auditing clerks
Bank tellers
Sewing machine operators, garment
Cleaners and servants, private household
Computer operators, except peripheral equipment
Billing, posting, and calculating machine operators
Duplicating, mail, and other office machine operators
Textile draw-out and winding machine operators and tenders
File clerks
Freight, stock, and material movers, hand
Farm workers
Machine tool cutting operators and tenders, metal and plastic
Central office operators
Central office and PBX installers and repairers
Electrical and electronic assemblers
Station installers and repairers, telephone
Personnel clerks, except payroll and timekeeping
Data entry keyers, except composing

-300   -250   -200   -150   -100   -50   0

Thousands

Chart 8. Projected Percent Growth in Employment by Level of Education and Training through 2005

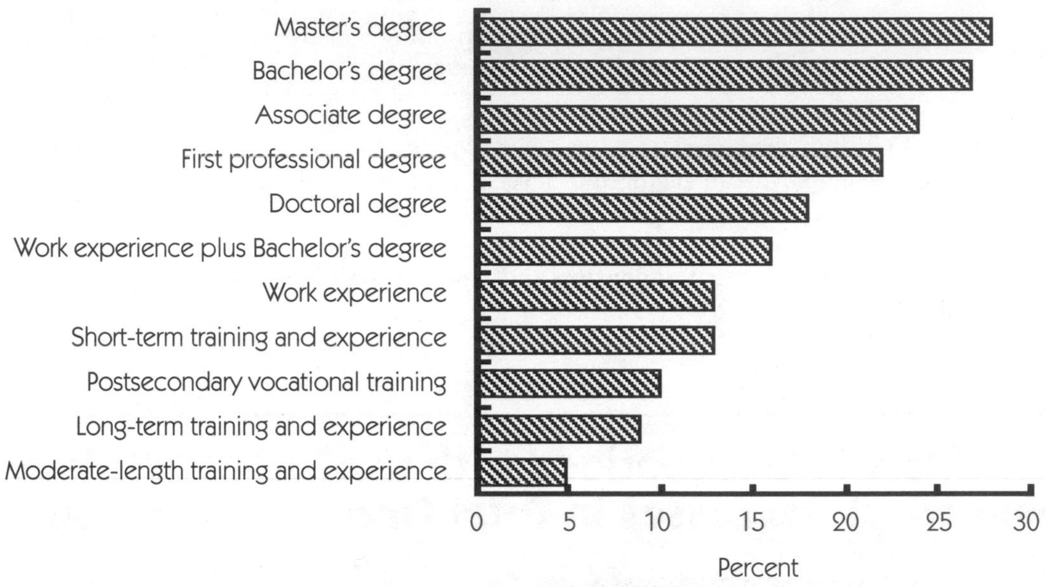

Master's degree
Bachelor's degree
Associate degree
First professional degree
Doctoral degree
Work experience plus Bachelor's degree
Work experience
Short-term training and experience
Postsecondary vocational training
Long-term training and experience
Moderate-length training and experience

0   5   10   15   20   25   30

Percent

▼ Occupations that require a bachelor's degree or above will average 23-percent growth, almost double the 12-percent growth projected for occupations that require less education and training.

▼ Occupations that pay above-average wages are projected to grow faster than occupations with below-average wages. Jobs with above-average wages are expected to account for 60 percent of employment growth. Jobs with higher earnings often require higher levels of education and training.

▼ Education is important in getting a high-paying job. However, many occupations— for example, registered nurses, blue-collar worker supervisors, electrical and electronic technicians/technologists, carpenters, and police and detectives—do not require a college degree yet offer higher-than-average earnings.

▼ Although high-paying jobs will be available without college training, most jobs that pay above-average wages will require a college degree.

▼ Educational services are projected to increase by 2.2 million jobs and to account for 1 out of every 8 jobs that will be added to the economy. Most jobs will be for teachers: In fact, teaching positions are projected to account for about 20 percent of all jobs available for college graduates.

▼ Projected employment growth of the occupations whose earnings rank in the top 25 percent was highly concentrated. Eight of the 146 occupations will account for about half of the new jobs: registered nurses, systems analysts, blue-collar worker supervisors, general managers and top executives, elementary school teachers, secondary school teachers, college faculty, and special education teachers.

Table 1. Jobs growing the fastest and those having the largest numerical increase in employment, by level of education and training

Fastest-growing occupations	Occupations having the largest numerical increase in employment

First professional degree

Chiropractors	Lawyers
Lawyers	Physicians
Physicians	Clergy
Clergy	Chiropractors
Podiatrists	Dentists

Doctoral degree

Medical scientists	College and university faculty
Biological scientists	Biological scientists
College and university faculty	Medical scientists
Mathematicians and all other mathematical scientists	Mathematicians and all other mathematical scientists

Master's degree

Operations research analysts	Management analysts
Speech-language pathologists and audiologists	Counselors
Management analysts	Speech-language pathologists and audiologists
Counselors	Psychologists
Urban and regional planners	Operations research analysts

Work experience plus bachelor's degree

Engineering, mathematics, and natural science managers	General managers and top executives
Marketing, advertising, and public relations managers	Financial managers
Artists and commercial artists	Marketing, advertising, and public relations managers
Financial managers	Engineering, mathematics, and natural science managers
Education administrators	Education administrators

Bachelor's degree

Systems analysts	Systems analysts
Computer engineers	Teachers, secondary school
Occupational therapists	Teachers, elementary school
Physical therapists	Teachers, special education
Special education teachers	Social workers

Associate degree

Paralegals	Registered nurses
Medical records technicians	Paralegals
Dental hygienists	Radiologic technologists and technicians

93

Table 1. (Continued)

Fastest-growing occupations	Occupations having the largest numerical increase in employment

Associate degree (Continued)

Respiratory therapists	Dental hygienists
Radiologic technologists and technicians	Medical records technicians

Postsecondary vocational training

Manicurists	Secretaries, except legal and medical
Surgical technologists	Licensed practical nurses
Data processing equipment repairers	Hairdressers, hair stylists, and cosmetologists
Dancers and choreographers	Legal secretaries
Emergency medical technicians	Medical secretaries

Work experience

Nursery and greenhouse managers	Marketing and sales worker supervisors
Lawn service managers	Clerical supervisors and managers
Food service and lodging managers	Food service and lodging managers
Clerical supervisors and managers	Instructors, adult education
Teachers and instructors, vocational and nonvocational training	Teachers and instructors, vocational and nonvocational training

Long-term training and experience (more than 12 months of on-the-job training)

Electronic pagination systems workers	Maintenance repairers, general utility
Correction officers	Correction officers
Securities and financial services sales workers	Automotive mechanics
Pattern makers and layout workers, fabric and apparel	Cooks, restaurant
Producers, directors, actors, and entertainers	Police patrol officers

Moderate-length training and experience
(1 to 12 months of combined on-the-job experience and informal training)

Physical and corrective therapy assistants and aides	Human services workers
Occupational therapy assistants and aides	Medical assistants
Human services workers	Instructors and coaches, sports and physical training
Medical assistants	Dental assistants
Detectives, except public	Painters and paper hangers, construction and maintenance

Short-term training and experience (up to a month of on-the-job experience)

Personal and home care aides	Cashiers
Home health aides	Janitors and cleaners, including maids and housekeepers
Amusement and recreation attendants	Salespersons, retail
Guards	Waiters and waitresses
Adjustment clerks	Home health aides

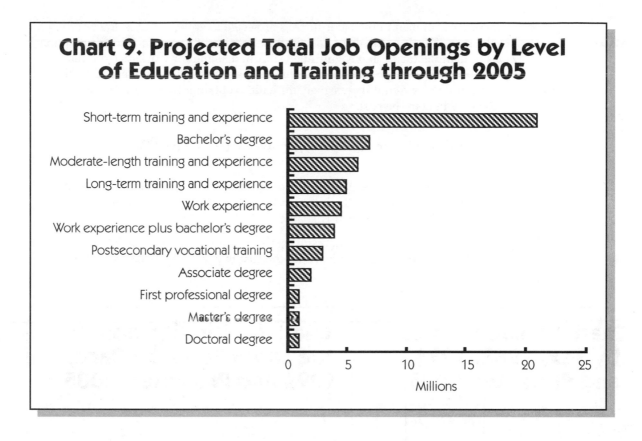

Chart 9. Projected Total Job Openings by Level of Education and Training through 2005

Short-term training and experience
Bachelor's degree
Moderate-length training and experience
Long-term training and experience
Work experience
Work experience plus bachelor's degree
Postsecondary vocational training
Associate degree
First professional degree
Master's degree
Doctoral degree

0   5   10   15   20   25
Millions

Jobs requiring the least education and training will provide the most openings but offer the lowest pay (see Chart 9).

▼ The distribution of jobs by education and training and by earnings will change little. Jobs requiring the least amount of education and training (and generally offering low pay) will continue to account for about 4 of every 10 jobs.

▼ Jobs that require moderate-length and short-term training and experience (the two categories requiring the least amount of education and training) will provide over half of total job openings through 2005.

The labor force will continue to grow faster than the population.

▼ As a result of the growing percentage of women entering the workforce, the labor force will grow slightly faster than the population through 2005.

Women will continue to make up an increasing share of the labor force (see Chart 10).

▼ Women are projected to represent a slightly greater proportion of the labor force in 2005 than they have in the recent past—increasing from 46 to 48 percent.

95

▼ The number of men in the labor force is projected to grow, but at a slower rate than in the past. This is partly due to declining employment in good-paying production jobs in manufacturing and a continued shift in demand for workers from the goods-producing sector to the service-producing sector. Men with less education and training may find it increasingly difficult to obtain jobs that pay as well as those they held in the past.

The labor force will become increasingly diverse (see Chart 11).

▼ The number of Hispanics, Asians, and other minorities will increase much faster than African-Americans and white non-Hispanics. African-Americans will increase faster than white non-Hispanics.

▼ Despite relatively slow growth, resulting in a declining share of the labor force, white non-Hispanics will still make up the vast majority of workers in 2005.

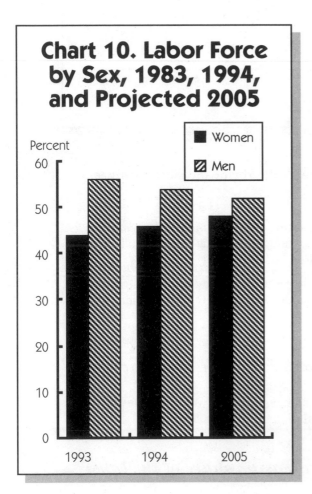

Chart 10. Labor Force by Sex, 1983, 1994, and Projected 2005

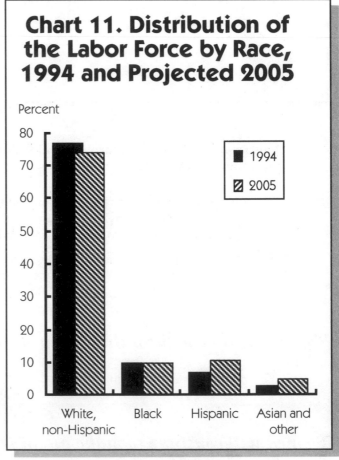

Chart 11. Distribution of the Labor Force by Race, 1994 and Projected 2005

Using the Job Matching Chart

The Job Matching Chart provides information on about 200 jobs. These are the most popular jobs in our economy—employing about 80 percent of all workers.

The jobs are organized into clusters of similar jobs. This allows you to identify major areas of interest and consider a variety of jobs within that cluster. Review each cluster so you can consider jobs you may have previously overlooked. If a job interests you, put a check mark by that job. After you have looked at the entire chart, go back and review more carefully the jobs that you checked. Circle those jobs that interest you most. These jobs will be worth learning more about.

The information in the chart are estimates and projections. They may or may not apply to a particular job or jobs in your region. Working conditions, skills required, pay, and other factors can vary greatly from one "similar" job to another. Projections for the future sometimes do not come true, or are very different from the conditions in your region.

Education Codes

Following are the education codes used in the chart.

Code	Description
H	High School Diploma
P	Postsecondary training
—	Typically either learned on the job or no formal training available

Employment Codes and Descriptions

The Job Matching Chart has four columns under its "Employment" heading. Each of these columns provides you with information that you should consider in making a career decision. The codes in these columns are described in the table below.

▼ **Average Earnings:** Jobs that require more education, training, or responsibility usually pay batter. But some lower-paying jobs could allow you to enjoy your work more. Most occupations have a wide range of earnings. Recent entrants and those in smaller cities often earn much less than the average.

▼ **Projected Growth:** Our economy is expected to create many new jobs in the years to come. Some jobs will grow more rapidly than others and some will decline. It is helpful to know if the demand for a job is likely to grow. However, you should not select a job because it is projected to grow quickly. Even where little growth is expected, new jobs are opening as employees retire or go on to other jobs.

▼ **Number of Openings:** Some occupations employ large numbers of people; others don't. A larger occupation may have many job openings even though it is not growing rapidly. This is often to replace workers who leave. Occupations with many openings may be easier to get, though they sometimes do not pay well.

▼ **Unemployment Rate:** Those seeking jobs in occupations with low rates of unemployment will often have fewer problems finding a job.

Code	Projected Growth	Average Earnings
VL	**Very Low:** within the lowest 20% of all occupations	$15 to $20,000/yr.
L	**Low:** within the next 20% of all occupations	$20 to 25,000/yr.
A	**Average:** within the middle or average 20% of all occupations	$26 to 35,000/yr.
H	**High:** within the next 20% of all occupations	$36 to 45,000/yr.
VH	**Very High:** within the highest 20% of all occupations	over $45,000

Skills and Working Conditions

The chart provides primary characteristics of a typical job in that occupation. Columns that are marked indicate that these skills or working conditions are typical. Not all jobs in an occupation are alike, so be careful to understand more about a job before you make important career choices.

Job Matching Chart

	EDUCATION AND TRAINING	SKILLS — WORKING WITH DATA/INFORMATION SKILLS			SKILLS — WORKING WITH PEOPLE SKILLS						WORKING WITH THINGS SKILLS		WORKING CONDITIONS						EMPLOYMENT			
		1. RESEARCHING AND COMPILING	2. ANALYZING AND EVALUATING	3. TROUBLESHOOTING	4. ARTISTIC EXPRESSION	5. INSTRUCTING	6. TREATING AND ADVISING	7. SUPERVISING	8. PERSUADING	9. PUBLIC CONTACT	10. MECHANICAL ABILITY	11. OPERATING A VEHICLE	12. REPETITIOUS	13. GEOGRAPHICALLY CONCENTRATED	14. MOBILE	15. PHYSICAL STAMINA	16. PART-TIME	17. IRREGULAR HOURS	18. AVERAGE EARNINGS	19. PROJECTED GROWTH	20. NUMBER OF OPENINGS	21. UNEMPLOYMENT RATE

Management and Financial Occupations

General Management Occupations

Occupation	Educ.	1	2	3	4	5	6	7	8	9	10	11	12	13	14	15	16	17	18	19	20	21
Administrative services managers	HPC		▼	▼			▼												H	L	VL	H
Employment interviewers/personnel specialists	P		▼					▼	▼										VH	H	VH	L
Hotel managers and assistants	C		▼	▼			▼		▼									▼	VL	VH	H	VH
Inspectors and compliance officers, except construction	C	▼	▼	▼					▼						▼				H	H	H	L
General managers and top executives	C		▼	▼				▼	▼										VH	A	L	H
Government chief executives and legislators	C		▼	▼			▼	▼	▼						▼		▼	▼	H	VL	A	VL
Personnel, training, and labor relations managers	C		▼	▼			▼		▼										VH	VH	H	L
Purchasing agents and managers	PC	▼	▼	▼				▼	▼										VH	A	H	VL

Financial Occupations

Occupation	Educ.	1	2	3	4	5	6	7	8	9	10	11	12	13	14	15	16	17	18	19	20	21
Accountants and auditors	C	▼	▼	▼															H	VH	VH	L
Budget analysts	C	▼	▼	▼															A	A	A	H
Cost estimators	C	▼	▼																A	L	L	H
Financial managers	C	▼	▼	▼				▼											VH	H	VH	L

Mathematical, Scientific, and Related Occupations

Mathematical Occupations

Occupation	Educ.	1	2	3	4	5	6	7	8	9	10	11	12	13	14	15	16	17	18	19	20	21
Actuaries	C	▼	▼																A	H	L	L
Computer systems analysts	C	▼	▼	▼															VH	VH	H	L
Computer programmers	C		▼	▼															H	H	H	L
Mathematicians	C	▼	▼																H	L	L	A
Operations research analysts	C	▼	▼	▼															VH	VH	H	L
Statistician clerks	C	▼	▼																A	VL	VL	L

Engineering Occupations

Occupation	Educ.	1	2	3	4	5	6	7	8	9	10	11	12	13	14	15	16	17	18	19	20	21
Drafters	P		▼	▼															H	A	H	L
Engineers (aerospace, chemical, civil, electrical and electronic industrial, mechanical, metallurgical, mining, nuclear, petroleum)	C	▼	▼	▼															VH	A	H	L
Engineering, science, and data processing managers	C	▼	▼	▼			▼												VH	H	H	L
All other engineering technicians and technologists	P	▼	▼	▼							▼								H	A	H	A

99

Job Matching Chart

	EDUCATION AND TRAINING	SKILLS — WORKING WITH DATA/INFORMATION SKILLS				SKILLS — WORKING WITH PEOPLE SKILLS					SKILLS — WORKING WITH THINGS SKILLS			WORKING CONDITIONS					EMPLOYMENT			
		1. RESEARCHING AND COMPILING	2. ANALYZING AND EVALUATING	3. TROUBLESHOOTING	4. ARTISTIC EXPRESSION	5. INSTRUCTING	6. TREATING AND ADVISING	7. SUPERVISING	8. PERSUADING	9. PUBLIC CONTACT	10. MECHANICAL ABILITY	11. OPERATING A VEHICLE	12. REPETITIOUS	13. GEOGRAPHICALLY CONCENTRATED	14. MOBILE	15. PHYSICAL STAMINA	16. PART-TIME	17. IRREGULAR HOURS	18. AVERAGE EARNINGS	19. PROJECTED GROWTH	20. NUMBER OF OPENINGS	21. UNEMPLOYMENT RATE

Scientists and Related Occupations

		1	2	3	4	5	6	7	8	9	10	11	12	13	14	15	16	17	18	19	20	21
Agricultural scientists	C	▼	▼																A	A	A	L
Biological scientists	C	▼	▼																H	VH	A	L
Foresters	C	▼	▼											▼	▼	▼			L	L	A	A
Physical scientists (chemists, geologists and geophysicists, meteorologists, physicists, astronomers)	C	▼	▼																H	A	A	L
Cartographers and geographers	C	▼	▼																			
Science and mathematics technicians	P	▼																	L	H	H	A

Architects and Surveyors

		1	2	3	4	5	6	7	8	9	10	11	12	13	14	15	16	17	18	19	20	21
Architects	C	▼	▼		▼														VH	H	H	VL
Landscape architects	C	▼	▼									▼							H	A	A	L
Surveyors	PC	▼	▼	▼											▼				A	A	A	A

Legal, Social Science, and Human Service Occupations

Legal Occupations (also see stenographers and court reporters under administrative support occupations)

		1	2	3	4	5	6	7	8	9	10	11	12	13	14	15	16	17	18	19	20	21
Lawyers	C	▼	▼	▼			▼		▼	▼									VH	VH	VH	VL
Paralegals	P	▼	▼							▼									L	H	H	L

Social Scientists and Urban Planners

		1	2	3	4	5	6	7	8	9	10	11	12	13	14	15	16	17	18	19	20	21
Anthropologists and archaeologists	C	▼	▼											▼	▼				H	A	L	A
Archivists, curators, and historians	C	▼	▼																H	A	L	A
Economists	C	▼	▼																VH	A	A	A
Marketing research analysts	C	▼	▼						▼										H	A	A	H
Psychologists	C	▼	▼	▼			▼		▼	▼									H	A	VH	VL
Urban and regional planners	C	▼	▼	▼					▼	▼									H	A	A	L
Sociologists	C	▼	▼							▼									H	L	L	H

Social and Recreation Workers

		1	2	3	4	5	6	7	8	9	10	11	12	13	14	15	16	17	18	19	20	21
Human services workers	PC	▼	▼				▼		▼							▼		▼	H	VH	VH	L
Recreation workers	HPC				▼					▼					▼	▼	▼	▼	VL	H	H	H

Job Matching Chart

| | EDUCATION AND TRAINING | SKILLS | | | | | | | | | | | | WORKING CONDITIONS | | | | | EMPLOYMENT | | | |
| | | WORKING WITH DATA/INFORMATION SKILLS | | | WORKING WITH PEOPLE SKILLS | | | | | | WORKING WITH THINGS SKILLS | | | | | | | | | | | |
		1. RESEARCHING AND COMPILING	2. ANALYZING AND EVALUATING	3. TROUBLESHOOTING	4. ARTISTIC EXPRESSION	5. INSTRUCTING	6. TREATING AND ADVISING	7. SUPERVISING	8. PERSUADING	9. PUBLIC CONTACT	10. MECHANICAL ABILITY	11. OPERATING A VEHICLE	12. REPETITIOUS	13. GEOGRAPHICALLY CONCENTRATED	14. MOBILE	15. PHYSICAL STAMINA	16. PART-TIME	17. IRREGULAR HOURS	18. AVERAGE EARNINGS	19. PROJECTED GROWTH	20. NUMBER OF OPENINGS	21. UNEMPLOYMENT RATE
Social workers	C	▼	▼	▼		▼			▼	▼					▼				H	VH	VH	L
Clergy	PC					▼	▼	▼	▼	▼					▼			▼	A	L	A	VL

Education and Related Occupations

Education Occupations

Adult education teachers	C	▼	▼	▼		▼	▼										▼	▼	A	H	H	L
Counselors	C		▼	▼		▼	▼		▼	▼									H	VH	H	VL
Education administrators	C		▼	▼		▼		▼	▼	▼									VH	H	H	VL
Kindergarten, elementary, and secondary school teachers	C		▼	▼		▼	▼										▼		H	VH	VH	VL
Preschool workers	HPC		▼			▼	▼		▼										L	H	H	L
Teacher aides and education assistants	HP					▼											▼		VL	VH	VH	A

Library Occupations

Librarians	C	▼		▼			▼										▼	▼	H	L	A	VL
Library assistants and bookmobile drivers	H						▼					▼			▼		▼	▼	VL	L	A	A
Library technicians	H	▼					▼										▼	▼	L	A	L	H

Health Care Occupations

Health diagnosing practitioners, chiropractors, dentists, optometrists, physicians, podiatrists, veterinarians	C	▼	▼	▼		▼	▼			▼							▼	▼	VH	H	A	VL
Health services managers	C	▼	▼	▼				▼	▼										VH	VH	H	L

Health Assessment and Treating Occupations

Dietitians and nutritionists	C		▼	▼		▼	▼			▼							▼		L	A	A	A
Occupational therapists	C		▼	▼		▼	▼			▼									A	VH	H	L
Pharmacists	C		▼	▼		▼	▼			▼									H	A	H	VL
Physical therapists	C		▼	▼		▼	▼			▼						▼	▼		H	VH	H	VL
Physician assistants	C		▼	▼		▼	▼			▼								▼	H	H	H	L
Recreational therapists	C		▼	▼		▼	▼			▼					▼	▼	▼		L	H	H	L
Registered nurses	PC		▼	▼		▼	▼			▼						▼	▼	▼	H	H	VH	VL
Respiratory therapists	PC		▼	▼		▼	▼			▼								A	VH	H		VL
Speech-language pathologists and audiologists	C		▼	▼		▼	▼			▼									H	VH	A	VL

101

Job Matching Chart

Column key:
- **EDUCATION AND TRAINING**
- **SKILLS — Working with Data/Information Skills:** 1. Researching and compiling · 2. Analyzing and evaluating · 3. Troubleshooting · 4. Artistic expression
- **Working with People Skills:** 5. Instructing · 6. Treating and advising · 7. Supervising · 8. Persuading · 9. Public contact
- **Working with Things Skills:** 10. Mechanical ability · 11. Operating a vehicle
- **WORKING CONDITIONS:** 12. Repetitious · 13. Geographically concentrated · 14. Mobile · 15. Physical stamina · 16. Part-time · 17. Irregular hours
- **EMPLOYMENT:** 18. Average earnings · 19. Projected growth · 20. Number of openings · 21. Unemployment rate

Health Technologists and Technicians

Occupation	Edu	1	2	3	4	5	6	7	8	9	10	11	12	13	14	15	16	17	18	19	20	21
Clinical laboratory technologists and technicians	PC		▼										▼						A	H	H	L
Dental hygienists	P					▼	▼			▼							▼		A	VH	H	VL
Opticians, dispensing and measuring	HP									▼									A	VH	A	A
EEG technologists	P	▼								▼			▼						L	VH	H	L
EKG technicians	H	▼								▼			▼						L	VH	H	L
Emergency medical technicians	P		▼	▼			▼			▼					▼		▼	▼	L	VH	H	L
Licensed practical nurses	P						▼			▼						▼	▼	▼	L	VH	VH	L
Medical record technicians	P	▼	▼															▼	L	VH	V	L
Nuclear medicine, radiologic technicians and technologists	P	▼								▼									H	VH	VH	VL
Radiological technologists	P	▼								▼			▼						L	VH	H	L
Surgical technicians	P						▼			▼									L	VH	H	L

Health Service Occupations

Occupation	Edu	1	2	3	4	5	6	7	8	9	10	11	12	13	14	15	16	17	18	19	20	21
Dental assistants	H						▼			▼							▼		VL	VH	H	A
Nursing aides, orderlies, and attendants	HP						▼			▼							▼	▼	VL	VH	VH	H
Homemaker-home health aides	HP						▼			▼					▼		▼		L	VH	VH	L

Communication, Visual Arts, and Performing Arts Occupations

Communications Occupations

Occupation	Edu	1	2	3	4	5	6	7	8	9	10	11	12	13	14	15	16	17	18	19	20	21
Broadcast technicians	P			▼							▼							▼	L	L	L	H
Marketing, advertising, and public relations managers	C		▼	▼	▼			▼	▼	▼				▼					VH	VH	VH	L
Public relations specialists and publicity writers	C	▼	▼	▼	▼				▼	▼				▼					VH	A	A	L
Radio and television announcers and newscasters	HPC	▼	▼		▼				▼	▼								▼	L	A	A	A
Reporters and correspondents	C	▼	▼		▼				▼	▼					▼			▼	L	A	L	A
Writers	PC	▼	▼		▼				▼	▼									L	H	H	L

Visual Arts Occupations

Occupation	Edu	1	2	3	4	5	6	7	8	9	10	11	12	13	14	15	16	17	18	19	20	21
Designers	HPC				▼					▼									A	A	L	H
Photographers and camera operators	P				▼					▼	▼						▼		A	H	H	L
Visual artists	HPC				▼														L	A	L	H

Job Matching Chart

	EDUCATION AND TRAINING	SKILLS — WORKING WITH DATA/INFORMATION SKILLS			4. ARTISTIC EXPRESSION	WORKING WITH PEOPLE SKILLS					WORKING WITH THINGS SKILLS		WORKING CONDITIONS						EMPLOYMENT			
		1. RESEARCHING AND COMPILING	2. ANALYZING AND EVALUATING	3. TROUBLESHOOTING	4. ARTISTIC EXPRESSION	5. INSTRUCTING	6. TREATING AND ADVISING	7. SUPERVISING	8. PERSUADING	9. PUBLIC CONTACT	10. MECHANICAL ABILITY	11. OPERATING A VEHICLE	12. REPETITIOUS	13. GEOGRAPHICALLY CONCENTRATED	14. MOBILE	15. PHYSICAL STAMINA	16. PART-TIME	17. IRREGULAR HOURS	18. AVERAGE EARNINGS	19. PROJECTED GROWTH	20. NUMBER OF OPENINGS	21. UNEMPLOYMENT RATE

Performing Artists

Occupation	EDU	1	2	3	4	5	6	7	8	9	10	11	12	13	14	15	16	17	18	19	20	21
Musicians	HC			▼			▼							▼	▼	▼	▼		L	L	A	A
Producers, directors, actors, and entertainers	PC	▼	▼	▼	▼	▼		▼	▼	▼					▼			▼	—	VH	H	VH

Sales and Related Occupations

Marketing, Retail and Sales Occupations

Occupation	EDU	1	2	3	4	5	6	7	8	9	10	11	12	13	14	15	16	17	18	19	20	21
Cashiers	H									▼			▼				▼	▼	VL	H	VH	VH
Counter and rental clerks	H									▼			▼				▼	▼	VL	VH	H	H
Manufacturers' and wholesale sales representatives	C	▼	▼	▼		▼			▼	▼					▼				L	L	L	H
Retail salesworkers	H								▼	▼							▼	▼	VL	H	VH	H
Securities and financial services sales workers	C	▼	▼				▼		▼	▼									VH	VH	H	L
Services sales representatives	H					▼			▼	▼									L	H	H	L
Travel agents	H	▼		▼					▼	▼							▼	▼	VL	VH	H	L
Wholesale and retail buyers	PC	▼	▼	▼				▼		▼									H	A	H	L

Insurance Occupations (also see adjusters, investigators, and collectors under administrative support occupations; and actuaries under mathematical occupations)

Occupation	EDU	1	2	3	4	5	6	7	8	9	10	11	12	13	14	15	16	17	18	19	20	21
Insurance sales workers	PC	▼	▼			▼			▼	▼									H	A	H	VL
Underwriters	PC	▼	▼																A	H	A	VL

Real Estate Occupations

Occupation	EDU	1	2	3	4	5	6	7	8	9	10	11	12	13	14	15	16	17	18	19	20	21
Property and real estate managers	C	▼	▼	▼				▼	▼	▼					▼				A	VH	H	L
Real estate agents, brokers, and appraisers	HP	▼	▼	▼			▼		▼	▼					▼		▼	▼	H	A	H	VL

Administrative Support Occupations

Occupation	EDU	1	2	3	4	5	6	7	8	9	10	11	12	13	14	15	16	17	18	19	20	21
Adjusters, investigators, and collectors	HPC	▼	▼							▼									L	A	H	L
Bank tellers	HP									▼			▼				▼		VL	VL	VL	A
Clerical supervisors and managers	HPC		▼	▼			▼												H	A	VH	VL
Computer operators	P			▼														▼	A	A	H	A
Credit clerks and authorizers	H	▼											▼						A	H	VH	A
Dispatchers	H			▼						▼			▼					▼	A	H	A	A
General office clerks	H																	▼	L	H	VH	A

103

Job Matching Chart

Occupation	EDUCATION AND TRAINING	1. RESEARCHING AND COMPILING	2. ANALYZING AND EVALUATING	3. TROUBLESHOOTING	4. ARTISTIC EXPRESSION	5. INSTRUCTING	6. TREATING AND ADVISING	7. SUPERVISING	8. PERSUADING	9. PUBLIC CONTACT	10. MECHANICAL ABILITY	11. OPERATING A VEHICLE	12. REPETITIOUS	13. GEOGRAPHICALLY CONCENTRATED	14. MOBILE	15. PHYSICAL STAMINA	16. PART-TIME	17. IRREGULAR HOURS	18. AVERAGE EARNINGS	19. PROJECTED GROWTH	20. NUMBER OF OPENINGS	21. UNEMPLOYMENT RATE
Postal mail carriers	H									▼		▼	▼		▼	▼	▼		H	H	H	VL
Mail clerks	H												▼						L	L	A	H
Material, recording, scheduling, and distributing occupations (stock clerks, shipping and receiving clerks)	H												▼						L	A	H	H
Messengers	H									▼		▼	▼	▼	▼	▼	▼		L	L	A	H
Postal service clerks	H									▼			▼				▼		H	L	L	A
Receptionists and other information clerks	H									▼			▼						VL	VH	VH	H
Records clerks (billing, bookkeeping, accounting, brokerage, file, order, payroll, and personnel clerks)	H	▼											▼						VL	L	H	L
Secretaries	H			▼						▼									L	A	VH	A
Stenographers	P												▼			▼			L	VL	VL	VL
Telephone operators	H									▼			▼					▼	L	VL	VL	H
Typists and word processors	H												▼						L	VL	VL	VL

Service Occupations

Protective Service Occupations

Occupation	EDUCATION AND TRAINING	1	2	3	4	5	6	7	8	9	10	11	12	13	14	15	16	17	18	19	20	21
Correction officers	H							▼										▼	A	VH	H	VL
Firefighters	H		▼					▼	▼						▼	▼		▼	A	H	H	L
Guards	H								▼					▼			▼	▼	VL	VH	VH	H
Police detectives and patrol officers	H	▼	▼	▼				▼	▼						▼	▼		▼	A	H	VH	VL

Food and Beverage Preparation and Service Occupations

Occupation	EDUCATION AND TRAINING	1	2	3	4	5	6	7	8	9	10	11	12	13	14	15	16	17	18	19	20	21
Chefs	P					▼		▼										▼	A	VH	VH	L
Cooks and other kitchen workers	H												▼			▼	▼		VL	VH	VH	L
Food and beverage service occupations	H									▼			▼			▼	▼		VL	VH	VH	L
Restaurant and food service managers	C		▼	▼				▼	▼									▼	L	VH	H	L

Personal Service and Facility Maintenance Occupations

Occupation	EDUCATION AND TRAINING	1	2	3	4	5	6	7	8	9	10	11	12	13	14	15	16	17	18	19	20	21
Animal caretakers, except farm	H														▼	▼		▼	L	VH	H	A
Barbers	P								▼				▼				▼	▼	L	VL	VL	VL
Gardeners and groundskeepers (except farm)	—											▼	▼		▼	▼	▼	▼	VL	VH	VH	VH
Janitors and cleaners	—												▼			▼	▼	▼	VL	A	VH	VH
Private household workers	—														▼	▼	▼	▼	VL	VL	VL	H

Job Matching Chart

Column key:

SKILLS — Working with Data/Information Skills: 1. Researching and Compiling · 2. Analyzing and Evaluating · 3. Troubleshooting · 4. Artistic Expression
Working with People Skills: 5. Instructing · 6. Treating and Advising · 7. Supervising · 8. Persuading · 9. Public Contact
Working with Things Skills: 10. Mechanical Ability · 11. Operating a Vehicle · 12. Repetitious
WORKING CONDITIONS: 13. Geographically Concentrated · 14. Mobile · 15. Physical Stamina · 16. Part-Time · 17. Irregular Hours
EMPLOYMENT: 18. Average Earnings · 19. Projected Growth · 20. Number of Openings · 21. Unemployment Rate

(Education and Training column at left.)

Agricultural, Forestry, Fishing, and Related Occupations

Occupation	Edu	1	2	3	4	5	6	7	8	9	10	11	12	13	14	15	16	17	18	19	20	21
Farm operators and managers	PC	▼	▼			▼						▼		▼	▼	▼		▼	L	A	A	A
Fishers, hunters, and trappers	—													▼	▼	▼	▼	▼	A	L	L	VH
Timber cutting and logging workers	—													▼	▼	▼		▼	VL	VL	VL	VH

Mechanics, Installers, and Repairers
(also see aircraft mechanics under air transportation occupations)

Occupation	Edu	1	2	3	4	5	6	7	8	9	10	11	12	13	14	15	16	17	18	19	20	21
Automotive body repairers	P			▼							▼					▼			A	H	H	A
Electronic equipment repairers (commercial and industrial electronic equipment, communications equipment, home entertainment, and telephone repairers)	P			▼						▼	▼				▼	▼			A	VL	L	L
Home appliance and power tool repairers	HP			▼						▼	▼				▼	▼			A	L	VL	L
Mechanics (automotive diesel, farm equipment, mobile heavy equipment, motorcycle, boat, small engine, and general maintenance mechanics)	P			▼						▼	▼					▼			L	A	H	L
Musical instrument repairers and tuners	—			▼						▼	▼				▼	▼			L	L	A	H
Vending machine servicers and repairers	H			▼						▼	▼				▼	▼			VL	L	A	A

Construction and Related Occupations

Occupation	Edu	1	2	3	4	5	6	7	8	9	10	11	12	13	14	15	16	17	18	19	20	21
Bricklayers and stonemasons	HP												▼		▼	▼			A	A	H	VH
Carpenters	HP														▼	▼			A	A	VH	VH
Carpet installers	HP													▼	▼	▼			L	A	A	H
Concrete masons and terazzo workers	HP														▼	▼			A	A	A	VH
Construction and building inspectors	HP		▼	▼					▼						▼	▼			A	A	A	L
Construction contractors and managers	PC	▼	▼	▼			▼	▼	▼						▼				H	L	VH	L
Drywall workers and lathers	HP														▼	▼			A	H	H	VH
Electricians	HP			▼							▼				▼	▼			H	H	VH	H
Elevator installers and repairers	H			▼							▼				▼	▼			A	A	A	L
Glaziers	HP														▼	▼			A	H	A	H
Heating, air-conditioning, and refrigeration technicians	HP			▼							▼				▼	▼			A	A	H	A
Insulation workers	HP													▼	▼	▼			L	H	A	VH
Line installers and cable splicers	—			▼							▼				▼	▼			H	VL	VL	L
Painters and paperhangers	HP													▼	▼	▼	▼		L	H	VH	L
Plasterers	HP													▼	▼	▼			H	A	L	H
Plumbers, pipefitters, and steamfitters	P			▼							▼				▼	▼			H	A	H	H

105

Job Matching Chart

	EDUCATION AND TRAINING	1. RESEARCHING AND COMPILING	2. ANALYZING AND EVALUATING	3. TROUBLESHOOTING	4. ARTISTIC EXPRESSION	5. INSTRUCTING	6. TREATING AND ADVISING	7. SUPERVISING	8. PERSUADING	9. PUBLIC CONTACT	10. MECHANICAL ABILITY	11. OPERATING A VEHICLE	12. REPETITIOUS	13. GEOGRAPHICALLY CONCENTRATED	14. MOBILE	15. PHYSICAL STAMINA	16. PART-TIME	17. IRREGULAR HOURS	18. AVERAGE EARNINGS	19. PROJECTED GROWTH	20. NUMBER OF OPENINGS	21. UNEMPLOYMENT RATE
Roofers	HP												▼		▼	▼			L	H	H	H
Roustabouts	—											▼		▼	▼	▼		▼	L	VL	VL	VH
Sheet-metal workers	P														▼	▼			L	A	H	H
Structural and reinforcing ironworkers	HP											▼		▼	▼	▼			H	A	A	VH
Hand tilesetters	HP												▼		▼	▼			A	H	L	VH

Production Occupations
Plant and Systems Operations

	EDUCATION AND TRAINING	1	2	3	4	5	6	7	8	9	10	11	12	13	14	15	16	17	18	19	20	21
Electric power generating plant operators and power dispatchers	H		▼	▼							▼							▼	A	L	L	H
Stationary engineers	H			▼							▼							▼	A	L	L	VL
Water and wastewater treatment plant operators	H	▼	▼	▼							▼							▼	A	H	A	VL

Printing Occupations

	EDUCATION AND TRAINING	1	2	3	4	5	6	7	8	9	10	11	12	13	14	15	16	17	18	19	20	21
Prepress workers	H		▼								▼							▼	A	VL	VL	H
Printing press operators	H		▼								▼		▼					▼	A	A	H	A
Bindery workers	H		▼								▼		▼						VL	A	L	A

Textile, Apparel, and Furnishing Occupations

	EDUCATION AND TRAINING	1	2	3	4	5	6	7	8	9	10	11	12	13	14	15	16	17	18	19	20	21
Apparel workers	—										▼								VL	L	H	L
Shoe and leather workers and repairers	—						▼				▼							▼	VL	L	L	H
Textile machinery operators	H		▼								▼		▼	▼				▼	L	L	A	A
Upholsterers	H																		L	L	L	A

Miscellaneous Production Occupations

	EDUCATION AND TRAINING	1	2	3	4	5	6	7	8	9	10	11	12	13	14	15	16	17	18	19	20	21
Blue-collar worker supervisors	H		▼			▼												▼	H	L	VH	L
Boilermakers	H	▼	▼								▼				▼	▼			A	VL	VL	H
Butcher, meat, and poultry cutters	H						▼						▼						L	VL	VL	H
Handlers, equipment cleaners, helpers, and laborers	—												▼			▼			VL	A	H	L
Industrial machinery repairers	P		▼	▼							▼				▼	▼		▼	H	L	H	A
Millwrights	P		▼	▼							▼				▼	▼			H	A	A	H
Industrial production managers	C		▼	▼				▼											VH	VL	A	L
Inspectors, testers, and graders	H		▼	▼									▼					▼	L	VL	L	H
Jewelers	P		▼							▼	▼								L	A	H	A

106

Job Matching Chart

	EDUCATION AND TRAINING	SKILLS — WORKING WITH DATA/INFORMATION SKILLS				SKILLS — WORKING WITH PEOPLE SKILLS					WORKING WITH THINGS SKILLS		WORKING CONDITIONS						EMPLOYMENT			
		1. RESEARCHING AND COMPILING	2. ANALYZING AND EVALUATING	3. TROUBLESHOOTING	4. ARTISTIC EXPRESSION	5. INSTRUCTING	6. TREATING AND ADVISING	7. SUPERVISING	8. PERSUADING	9. PUBLIC CONTACT	10. MECHANICAL ABILITY	11. OPERATING A VEHICLE	12. REPETITIOUS	13. GEOGRAPHICALLY CONCENTRATED	14. MOBILE	15. PHYSICAL STAMINA	16. PART-TIME	17. IRREGULAR HOURS	18. AVERAGE EARNINGS	19. PROJECTED GROWTH	20. NUMBER OF OPENINGS	21. UNEMPLOYMENT RATE
Machinists	P			▼							▼							▼	A	L	H	A
Tool and die makers	P			▼							▼							▼	H	L	L	L
Metal and plastics working machine operators	H			▼							▼		▼					▼	L	VL	VL	VH
Numerical control machine tool operators	H			▼							▼		▼					▼	H	A	L	L
Painting and coating machine operators	—										▼		▼						L	L	VL	VH
Photographic process workers	H										▼		▼				▼	▼	VL	A	A	A
Precision assemblers	H			▼							▼		▼						VL	L	L	A
Tool programmers, numerical control	PC	▼	▼								▼								H	H	L	L
Welders, cutters, and welding machine operators	P										▼		▼			▼		▼	A	L	A	VH
Woodworking occupations	H										▼		▼						L	A	A	VH

Transportation Occupations

Air Transportation Occupations

	EDU	1	2	3	4	5	6	7	8	9	10	11	12	13	14	15	16	17	18	19	20	21
Aircraft pilots	C		▼									▼			▼			▼	VH	H	A	H
Air traffic controllers	HPC	▼	▼															▼	H	L	L	L
Aircraft mechanics and engine specialists	P		▼				▼									▼		▼	VH	H	L	L
Flight attendants	HP		▼				▼								▼			▼	VL	L	H	H

Ground Transportation Occupations

	EDU	1	2	3	4	5	6	7	8	9	10	11	12	13	14	15	16	17	18	19	20	21
Busdrivers	H		▼			▼					▼	▼			▼		▼	▼	A	VH	VH	A
Material moving equipment operators	HP										▼	▼			▼				A	L	A	VH
Rail transportation occupations	H		▼								▼				▼			▼	A	VL	VL	A
Truck drivers	H		▼								▼	▼			▼	▼		▼	A	H	VH	H

Water Transportation Occupations

	EDU	1	2	3	4	5	6	7	8	9	10	11	12	13	14	15	16	17	18	19	20	21
Marine engineers and captains	C		▼				▼				▼	▼			▼			▼	H	L	VL	VH
Mates and seamen	H		▼								▼					▼	▼	▼	L	L	VL	VH

Chapter 5 Endnote

1. The information in this section is based on projections provided by the U.S. Department of Labor. It covers the time period from 1994 through 2005. Due to delays in the Department's collecting and publishing of data (typically a two-year delay), this is the latest information available at the time of this writing. While it may seem like old data by the time you read this, it points the way to the future. Most labor market trends do not change quickly, and the trends noted here are likely to be true for many years. Additional education and training, for example, will be good to have over the next hundred years, and not just for the next decade.

chapter

Getting More Information on Jobs, Training, and Education

In this chapter, we will review sources of information on jobs that interest you. In the second section, we'll explore sources of additional training and education.

At this point, you should have a good idea of the types of jobs that interest you. In Chapter 5, you identified major jobs of interest in the Job Matching Chart. To make a good career decision, you need to learn more about these and similar jobs. You might eliminate a job based on what you learn about its pay, education or training requirements, working conditions, or other factors.

Eliminating a job from consideration is just as important as identifying one. The more you know about a job, the better you are able to make a good decision. Some people invest years of time and effort going to school or working in a job, only to find that it is not what they really want to do. This chapter will give you sources of information to use in making a career decision. Researching jobs that interest you will take some time, but it can save you much more in the end.

The *Occupational Outlook Handbook*

There are many sources of information on careers. One of the very best is the *Occupational Outlook Handbook* (the *OOH*). Published by the U.S. Department of Labor, the *OOH* is an excellent source of information on the jobs listed in the Job Matching Chart in Chapter 5.

The *OOH* is revised every two years, so look for the current edition. Most libraries have one, as do many schools and vocational counselors. You can also find it at many bookstores, along with a book with the same information titled *America's Top 300 Jobs*. Many computerized career information sources also include information from the *OOH*.

The *OOH* provides brief descriptions of all major jobs in the U.S. workforce. The descriptions are well-written and packed with information. Each job description contains these sections:

▼ Nature of the Work

▼ Working Conditions

▼ Employment

▼ Training, Other Qualifications, and Advancement

▼ Job Outlook

▼ Earnings

▼ Related Occupations

▼ Sources of Additional Information

Although the descriptions are short, they are full of data that can be of great value. Three sample job descriptions from the *OOH* are presented later in this chapter to give you an idea of their usefulness.

Tips on Using the *OOH* Descriptions

The Job Matching Chart should have given you good ideas of which jobs you want to learn more about. Descriptions for these jobs can be found in the *OOH,* and you should read them carefully. The *OOH* is organized into groups of related jobs, allowing you to easily find other jobs that might interest you. You should read the OOH descriptions of these related jobs too.

You should also use the *OOH* to review jobs you have held in the past. Most likely, some of the skills required for your pervious job (transferable skills) are needed in the job you now seek. Use the *OOH* description to identify skills needed in your new job and look for similar skills in your previous jobs. You can mention these skills in an interview to support your ability to do the new job.

As an example, let's assume that at one time you waited on tables in a restaurant. You now want a job as a secretary. Maybe in your interviews you had planned to skip over your experience as a waiter or waitress because it didn't seem relevant to your new job. But skills you used in your old job often *do* relate to your new objective.

Look at the *OOH* descriptions later in this section. Notice that similar skills are mentioned for *both* jobs. For example, in the description for secretaries, you will read:

> " Because secretaries must be tactful in their dealings with many different people, employers also look for good interpersonal skills. Discretion, judgment, organizational ability, and initiative are especially important. "

Now look at the description for food services workers, including waiters and waitresses. You will find the need for similar skills:

> 66 ... expected to provide fast and efficient, yet courteous, service ... During busy dining periods, they are under pressure to serve customers quickly and efficiently. 99

Armed with such information, you could make this statement:

> 66 In a previous job, I worked with large numbers of customers—more than 1,000 per week. I learned to take care of their needs quickly and efficiently while maintaining a friendly and professional manner. 99

If you look at the description for computer programmers, you will find similar transferable skills. For example, computer programmers, waiters and waitresses, and secretaries all must work with accuracy under pressure. There are usually similarities between any two jobs. It's often helpful to review a job that interests you and list all the skills necessary to do it well. Then create a similar list for your past jobs to help you identify transferable skills.

The *OOH* can be used in other ways during a job search. For example, once you know the kind of job you will be seeking, carefully review the *OOH* descriptions for related jobs. The descriptions provide a great deal of information on the required skills, salary ranges, and other details that can help you in your interviews.

Sample Job Descriptions from the *OOH*

I've selected three job descriptions from the *OOH* for you to review. Most people are familiar with the basic tasks of secretaries and food service workers. Even so, it is likely you will learn new things about these jobs. The computer programmer description is included as an example of a more technical job.

I have made very minor changes in the descriptions from the way they actually appear in the *OOH*. Each of the descriptions in the *OOH* provides similar information, and I urge you to read the *OOH* descriptions for the jobs that interest you.

As you review the descriptions of jobs that interest you, make notes on things you like or do not like about each. Also note things that you will need to do (such as getting more training or education) in order to enter these jobs. Later in this chapter you will find a worksheet to help you organize information about the jobs that most interest you. Doing this *will* help you make better plans for your career and for any additional training or education.

Secretaries

Nature of the Work

Secretarial work continues to evolve along with new office automation and organizational restructuring. In many cases, secretaries have assumed new responsibilities and learned to operate different office equipment. In the midst of these changes, though, their central responsibilities remain much as they were. Most organizations still employ secretaries to perform and coordinate office activities and to ensure that information gets disseminated to staff and clients. Managers, professionals, and other support staff still rely on them to keep administrative operations under control.

Secretaries are responsible for a variety of administrative and clerical duties that are necessary to run and maintain organizations efficiently. They schedule appointments, give information to callers, organize and maintain files, complete forms, and take dictation. They may also type letters, make travel arrangements, or contact clients. In addition, secretaries operate office equipment like facsimile machines, photocopiers, and telephones with voice mail capabilities.

Secretaries increasingly use personal computers to run spreadsheet, word processing, data base management, desktop publishing, and graphics programs—tasks previously handled by managers and professionals. Because they are often relieved from dictation and typing, they can support several members of the professional staff. Secretaries sometimes work in clusters of three or four so that they can work more flexibly and share their expertise.

Executive secretaries or administrative assistants perform fewer clerical tasks than lower-level secretaries. In addition to receiving visitors, arranging conference calls, and answering letters, they may handle more complex responsibilities like conducting research, preparing statistical reports, training employees, and supervising other clerical staff.

Some secretaries do highly specialized work that requires a knowledge of technical terminology and procedures. Further specialization in various types of law is common among legal secretaries, for example. They prepare correspondence and legal papers such as summonses, complaints, motions, and subpoenas under the supervision of an attorney. They also may review legal journals and assist in other ways with legal research. Medical secretaries comprise another type of specialized secretary. These workers transcribe dictation, prepare correspondence, and assist physicians or medical scientists with reports, speeches, articles, and conference proceedings. They also record simple medical histories, arrange for patients to be hospitalized, and order supplies. Most medical secretaries need to be familiar with insurance rules, billing practices, and hospital or laboratory procedures. Other technical secretaries assist engineers or scientists. They may prepare correspondence, maintain the technical library, and gather and edit materials for scientific papers.

Working Conditions

Secretaries usually work in offices with other professionals or in schools, hospitals, or doctors' offices. Their jobs often involve sitting for long periods. If they spend a lot of time typing, particularly at a video display terminal, they may encounter problems of eyestrain, stress, and repetitive motion problems such as carpal tunnel syndrome.

Office work lends itself to alternative or flexible working arrangements, like telecommuting, and one secretary in six works part-time. In addition, a significant number of secretaries work as temporaries. A few participate in job sharing arrangements in which two people divide responsibility for a single job. The majority of secretaries, however, are full-time employees who work a standard 40-hour week.

Employment

Secretaries hold over 3.3 million jobs, making this one of the largest occupations in the U.S. economy. The following tabulation shows the distribution of employment by secretarial specialty.

Secretaries, total: 3,349,000

    Legal secretaries: 281,000

    Medical secretaries: 226,000

    Secretaries, except legal and medical: 2,842,000

Secretaries are employed in organizations of every description. About one-half of all secretaries are employed in firms providing services, ranging from education and health to legal and business services. Others work for firms that engage in manufacturing, construction, wholesale and retail trade, transportation, and communications. Banks, insurance companies, investment firms, and real estate firms are important employers, as are federal, state, and local government agencies.

Training, Other Qualifications, and Advancement

High school graduates may qualify for secretarial positions, provided they have basic office skills. Secretaries should be proficient in keyboarding and good at spelling, punctuation, grammar, and oral communication. Shorthand is necessary for some positions. Knowledge of word processing, spreadsheet, and database management programs is becoming increasingly important to most employers. Because secretaries must be tactful in their dealings with many different people, employers also look for good interpersonal skills. Discretion, judgment, organizational ability, and initiative are especially important for higher-level secretarial positions.

As office automation continues to evolve, retraining and continuing education will remain an integral part of many jobs. Continuing changes in the office environment have increased the demand for secretaries who are adaptable and versatile. Secretaries may have to attend classes to learn to operate new office equipment, such as word processing equipment, information storage systems, personal computers, or new updated software packages.

The skills needed for a secretarial job can be acquired in various ways. Secretarial training ranges from high school vocational education programs that teach office practices, shorthand, and keyboarding skills to one- to two-year programs in secretarial science offered by business schools, vocational-technical institutes, and community colleges. Many temporary help agencies provide formal training in computer and keyboarding skills. These skills are most often acquired, however, through instruction offered at the workplace by other employees or by equipment and software vendors. Specialized training programs are available for students planning to become medical or legal secretaries or office automation specialists.

Testing and certification for entry-level office skills is available through the Office Proficiency Assessment and Certification (OPAC) program offered by Professional Secretaries International (PSI). As secretaries gain experience, they can earn the designation Certified Professional Secretary (CPS) by passing a series of examinations given by the Institute for Certifying Secretaries, a department of PSI. This designation is recognized by many employers as the mark of excellence for senior-level office professionals. Similarly, those without experience who want to be certified as a legal support professional may be certified as an Accredited Legal Secretary (ALS) by the Certifying Board of the National Association of Legal Secretaries. They also administer an examination to certify a legal secretary with three years of experience as a Professional Legal Secretary (PLS).

Advancement for secretaries generally comes about by promotion to a secretarial position with more responsibilities. Qualified secretaries who broaden their knowledge of the company's operations and enhance their skills may be promoted to other positions such as senior or executive secretary, clerical supervisor, or office manager.

Secretaries with word processing experience can advance to jobs as word processing trainers, supervisors, or managers within their own firms or in a secretarial or word processing service bureau. Their experience as a secretary can lead to jobs such as instructor or sales representative with manufacturers of word processing or computer equipment. With additional training, many legal secretaries become legal assistants and paralegals.

113

Job Outlook

Projected employment growth for secretaries varies by occupational specialty. Growth in the legal services and health services industries will drive faster-than-average employment growth for legal and medical secretaries through the year 2005. Employment of the 85 percent of secretaries who are not legal or medical secretaries, however, is expected to grow more slowly than the average for all occupations. Nevertheless, employment opportunities should be quite plentiful, especially for well-qualified and experienced secretaries, who, according to many employers, are in short supply. The very large size of the occupation, coupled with a moderate turnover rate, will generate several hundred thousand secretarial positions each year as experienced workers transfer to other occupations or leave the labor force.

The major factor limiting employment growth for most secretaries is the widespread application of new office automation. Secretaries have become more productive with the help of word processing machines, personal computers, electronic mail, scanners, facsimile machines, and voice message systems. These technologies will continue to be purchased by firms, ensuring that employment growth for secretaries will lag behind the rapidly growing amount of office work.

The use of automated equipment is also changing the work flow in many offices. Administrative duties are being reassigned and the functions of entire departments are being restructured. In some cases, such traditional secretarial duties as typing or keyboarding, filing, copying, and accounting are being assigned to workers in other units or departments. In some law offices and physicians' offices, for example, paralegals and medical assistants are assuming some tasks formerly done by secretaries. Professionals and managers increasingly do their own word processing rather than submit the work to secretaries and other support staff. In addition, there is a trend in many offices for groups of professionals and managers to "share" secretaries. The traditional arrangement of one secretary per manager is becoming less prevalent; instead, secretaries increasingly support systems or units. This approach often means that secretaries assume added responsibilities and are seen as valuable members of a team, but it also contributes to slower rates of employment growth.

Developments in office technology are certain to continue, and they will bring about further changes in the secretary's work environment. However, many secretarial job duties are of a personal, interactive nature and, therefore, not easily automated. Duties such as planning conferences, receiving clients, and transmitting staff instructions require tact and communication skills. Because automated equipment cannot substitute for these personal skills, secretaries will continue to play a key role in the office activities of most organizations.

Earnings

Based on a survey of metropolitan areas, the average annual salary for all secretaries was $26,700. Salaries vary a great deal, however, reflecting differences in skill, experience, and level of responsibility, ranging from $19,100 to $38,400.

Salaries in different parts of the country also vary; earnings generally are lowest in Southern cities, and highest in Northern and Western cities. In addition, salaries vary by industry; salaries of secretaries tend to be highest in transportation, legal services, and public utilities, and lowest in retail trade and finance, insurance, and real estate.

The starting salary for inexperienced secretaries in the federal government was $16,700 a year. Beginning salaries were slightly higher in selected areas where the prevailing local pay level was higher. All secretaries employed by the federal government averaged about $25,800.

Related Occupations

A number of other workers type, record information, and process paperwork. Among these are bookkeepers, receptionists, stenographers, personnel clerks, typists and word processors, legal assistants, medical assistants, and medical record technicians. A growing number of secretaries share in managerial and human resource responsibilities. Occupations requiring these skills include clerical supervisor, systems manager, office manager, and human resource officer.

Sources of Additional Information

For career information, contact:

> Professional Secretaries International, P.O. Box 20404, Kansas City, MO 64195-0404. (Phone: 1-816-891-6600.)

Persons interested in careers as legal secretaries can request information from:

> National Association of Legal Secretaries (International), 2250 East 73rd St., Suite 550, Tulsa, OK 74136.

State employment offices can provide information about job openings for secretaries.

Food and Beverage Service Workers

Nature of the Work

Whether they work in small, informal diners or large, elegant restaurants, all food and beverage service workers deal with customers. The quality of service they deliver determines in part whether or not patrons will return.

Waiters and waitresses take customers' orders, serve food and beverages, prepare itemized checks, and sometimes accept payments. The manner in which they perform their tasks varies considerably, depending on the establishment where they work. In coffee shops, they are expected to provide fast and efficient, yet courteous, service. In fine restaurants, where gourmet meals are accompanied by attentive formal service, waiters and waitresses serve the meal at a more leisurely pace and offer more personal service to patrons. For example, they may recommend a certain kind of wine as a complement to a particular entree, explain how various items on the menu are prepared, or prepare some salads and other special dishes at table side.

Depending on the type of restaurant, waiters and waitresses may perform additional duties generally associated with other food and beverage service occupations. These tasks may include escorting guests to tables, serving customers seated at counters, setting up and clearing tables, or cashiering. However, larger or more formal restaurants frequently hire staff to perform these duties, allowing their waiters and waitresses to concentrate on customer service.

Bartenders fill the drink orders that waiters and waitresses take from customers seated in the restaurant or lounge, as well as orders from customers seated at the bar. They prepare standard mixed drinks and, occasionally, are asked to mix drinks to suit a customer's taste. Most bartenders know dozens of drink recipes and are able to mix drinks accurately, quickly, and without waste, even during the busiest periods. Besides mixing and serving drinks, bartenders collect payment, operate the cash register, clean up after customers have left, and on occasion serve food items to customers seated at the bar.

Bartenders who work at service bars have little contact with customers. They work at small bars in restaurants, hotels, and clubs where drinks are served only by waiters and waitresses. However, the majority who work in eating and drinking establishments directly serve and socialize with patrons.

Some establishments, especially larger ones, use automatic equipment to mix drinks of varying complexity at the push of a button. However, bartenders still must be efficient and knowledgeable

115

in case the equipment malfunctions or a customer requests a drink not handled by the equipment. Most customers frequent drinking establishments for the friendly atmosphere and would rather have their drinks prepared by a bartender than a lifeless machine.

Bartenders usually are responsible for ordering and maintaining an inventory of liquor, mixes, and other bar supplies. They form attractive displays out of the bottles and glassware, and wash the glassware and utensils after each use.

Hosts and hostesses try to evoke a good impression of the restaurant by warmly welcoming guests. They courteously direct patrons to where they may leave coats and other personal items, and indicate where they may wait until their table is ready. Hosts and hostesses assign guests to tables suitable for the size of their group, escort them to their seats, and provide menus.

Hosts and hostesses are restaurants' personal representatives to patrons. They try to ensure that the service is prompt and courteous and that the meal meets expectations. Hosts and hostesses schedule dining reservations, arrange parties, and organize any special services that are required. In some restaurants, they also act as cashiers.

Dining room attendants and bartender helpers assist waiters, waitresses, and bartenders by keeping the serving area stocked with supplies, cleaning tables, and removing dirty dishes to the kitchen. They replenish the supply of clean linens, dishes, silverware, and glasses in the restaurant dining room, and keep the bar stocked with glasses, liquor, ice, and drink garnishes. Bartender helpers also keep the bar equipment clean and wash glasses. Dining room attendants set tables with clean tablecloths, napkins, silverware, glasses, and dishes and serve ice water, rolls, and butter to patrons. At the conclusion of the meal, they remove dirty dishes and soiled linens from the tables. Cafeteria attendants stock serving tables with food, trays, dishes, and silverware and may carry trays to dining tables for patrons.

Counter attendants take orders and serve food at counters. In cafeterias, they serve food displayed on counters and steam tables as requested by patrons, carve meat, dish out vegetables, ladle sauces and soups, and fill beverages. In lunchrooms and coffee shops, counter attendants take orders from customers seated at the counter, transmit the orders to the kitchen, and pick up and serve the food when it is ready. They also fill cups with coffee, soda, and other beverages and prepare fountain specialties such as milkshakes and ice cream sundaes. They prepare some short-order items, such as sandwiches and salads, and wrap or place orders in containers for carry out. Counter attendants also clean counters, write up itemized checks, and accept payment.

Fast-food workers take orders from customers at counters or drive-through windows at fast-food restaurants. They get the ordered beverage and food items, serve them to the customer, and accept payment. Many fast-food workers also cook and package French fries, make coffee, and fill beverage cups using a drink-dispensing machine.

Working Conditions

Food and beverage service workers are on their feet most of the time and often carry heavy trays of food, dishes, and glassware. During busy dining periods, they are under pressure to serve customers quickly and efficiently. The work is relatively safe, but care must be taken to avoid slips, falls, and burns.

Although some food and beverage service workers work 40 hours or more a week, the majority are employed part-time—a larger proportion than in almost any other occupation. The majority of those working part-time schedules do so on a voluntary basis. The wide range in dining hours creates work opportunities attractive to homemakers, students, and other individuals seeking supplemental income. Many food and beverage service workers are expected to work evenings, weekends, and holidays. Some work split shifts—that is, they work for several hours during the middle of the day, take a few hours off in the afternoon, and then return to their jobs for the evening hours.

Employment

Food and beverage service workers held more than 4.5 million jobs. Waiters and waitresses held over 1.8 million of these jobs; counter attendants and fast-food workers, more than 1.6 million; dining room and cafeteria attendants and bartender helpers, 416,000; bartenders, 373,000; and hosts and hostesses, 248,000.

Restaurants, coffee shops, bars, and other retail eating and drinking places employed two-thirds of all food and beverage service workers. Of the remainder, nearly half worked in hotels and other lodging places, and others in bowling alleys, casinos, and country clubs and other membership organizations.

Jobs are located throughout the country but are typically plentiful in large cities and tourist areas. Vacation resorts offer seasonal employment, and some workers alternate between summer and winter resorts instead of remaining in one area the entire year.

Training, Other Qualifications, and Advancement

There are no specific educational requirements for food and beverage service jobs. Although many employers prefer to hire high school graduates for waiter and waitress, bartender, and host and hostess positions, completion of high school is generally not required for fast-food workers, counter attendants, and dining room attendants and bartender helpers. For many people, a job as a food and beverage service worker serves as a source of immediate income rather than a career. Many entrants to these jobs are in their late teens or early twenties and have a high school education or less. Usually, they have little or no work experience. Many are full-time students or homemakers. Food and beverage service jobs are a major source of part-time employment for high school students.

Most employers place an emphasis on personal qualities. Food and beverage service workers are in close contact with the public, so they should be well-spoken and have a neat and clean appearance. They should enjoy dealing with all kinds of people, possess a pleasant disposition and a healthy sense of humor. State laws often require that food and beverage service workers obtain health certificates showing that they are free of communicable diseases.

Waiters and waitresses need a good memory to avoid confusing customers' orders and to recall the faces, names, and preferences of frequent patrons. They should be good at arithmetic so they can total bills without the assistance of a calculator or cash register. In restaurants specializing in foreign foods, knowledge of a foreign language is helpful. Prior experience waiting on tables is preferred by restaurants and hotels that have rigid table service standards. Jobs at these establishments often have higher earnings, but may also have higher educational requirements than less formal establishments.

Generally, bartenders must be at least 21 years of age, and employers prefer to hire people who are 25 or older. They should be familiar with state and local laws concerning the sale of alcoholic beverages.

Most food and beverage service workers pick up their skills on the job by observing and working with more experienced workers. Some employers, particularly some fast-food restaurants, use self-instruction programs to teach new employees food preparation and service skills through audiovisual presentations and instructional booklets. Some public and private vocational schools, restaurant associations, and large restaurant chains also provide classroom training in a generalized food service curriculum.

Some bartenders acquire their skills by attending a bartending or vocational and technical school. These programs often include instruction on state and local laws and regulations, cocktail recipes, attire and conduct, and stocking a bar. Some of these schools help their graduates find jobs.

Due to the relatively small size of most food-serving establishments, opportunities for promotion are limited. After gaining some experience, some dining room and cafeteria attendants and bartender helpers are able to advance to waiter, waitress, or bartender jobs. For waiters, waitresses, and bartenders, advancement usually is limited to finding a job in a larger restaurant or bar where prospects for tip earnings are better. Some bartenders open their own businesses. Some hosts and hostesses and waiters and waitresses advance to supervisory jobs, such as maitre d'hotel, dining

117

room supervisor, or restaurant manager. In larger restaurant chains, food and beverage service workers who excel at their work are often invited to enter the company's formal management training program.

Job Outlook

Job openings for food and beverage service workers are expected to be abundant through the year 2005. Most openings will arise from the need to replace the high proportion of workers who leave this very large occupation each year. There is substantial movement into and out of the occupation because the education and training requirements are minimal, and the predominance of part-time jobs is attractive to people seeking a short-term source of income rather than a career. Many of these workers simply move to other occupations, while others stop working to assume household responsibilities or to attend school.

Employment of food and beverage service occupations is expected to grow about as fast as the average for all occupations through the year 2005. Since a significant proportion of food and beverage sales by eating and drinking places is associated with the overall level of economic activity, sales and employment will increase with the growth of the economy. Growth in demand also will stem from population growth, rising personal incomes, and increased leisure time. Since it is common for both husband and wife to be in the workforce, families may increasingly find dining out a convenience.

Growth of the various types of food and beverage service jobs is expected to vary greatly. As the composition of the nation's population becomes older, diners are expected to patronize full-service restaurants increasingly, spurring growth in demand for waiters and waitresses and hosts and hostesses. However, little change in the employment of dining room attendants is expected as waiters and waitresses increasingly assume their duties. The employment of bartenders is expected to decline as drinking of alcoholic beverages outside the home—particularly cocktails—continues to drop.

Workers under the age of 25 have traditionally filled a significant proportion of food and beverage service jobs, particularly in fast-food restaurants. The pool of these young workers in the labor force is expected to shrink through the 1990s, but begin to grow after the year 2000. To attract and retain workers, many employers will be forced to offer higher wages, better benefits, more training, and increased opportunities for advancement and full-time employment.

Because potential earnings are greatest in popular restaurants and fine dining establishments, keen competition is expected for the limited number of jobs in these restaurants.

Earnings

Food and beverage service workers derive their earnings from a combination of hourly wages and customer tips. Their wages and the amount of tips they receive varies greatly, depending on the type of job and establishment. For example, fast-food workers and hosts and hostesses generally do not receive tips, so their wage rates may be higher than those of waiters and waitresses, who may earn more from tips than from wages. In some restaurants, waiters and waitresses contribute a portion of their tips to a tip pool, which is distributed among many of the establishment's other food and beverage service workers and kitchen staff. Tip pools allow workers who normally do not receive tips, such as dining room attendants, to share in the rewards for a well-served meal.

Median weekly earnings (including tips) of full-time waiters and waitresses were about $256. The middle 50 percent earned between $188 and $338; the top 10 percent earned at least $430 a week. For most waiters and waitresses, higher earnings are primarily the result of receiving more in tips rather than higher hourly wages. Tips generally average between 10 and 20 percent of guests' checks, so waiters and waitresses working in busy, expensive restaurants earn the most.

Full-time bartenders had median weekly earnings (including tips) of about $299. The middle 50 percent earned from $226 and $395; the top 10 percent earned at least $514 a week. Like waiters and waitresses, bartenders employed in public bars may receive more than half of their earnings as tips. Service bartenders are often paid higher hourly wages to offset their lower tip earnings.

Median weekly earnings (including tips) of full-time dining room attendants and bartender helpers were about $228. The middle 50 percent earned between $182 and $304; the top 10 percent earned over $446 a week. Most received over half of their earnings as wages; the rest was their share of the proceeds from tip pools.

Full-time counter attendants and fast-food workers had median weekly earnings (including any tips) of about $204. The middle 50 percent earned between $160 and $266, while the highest 10 percent earned over $324 a week. Although some counter attendants receive part of their earnings as tips, fast-food workers generally do not.

In establishments covered by federal law, workers often are paid the minimum wage. Federal law permits employers to credit an employee's tip earnings toward the minimum hourly wage, up to an amount equaling 45 percent of the minimum, and some employers exercise this right. Employers are also permitted to deduct from wages the cost, or fair value, of any meals or lodging provided. However, many employers provide free meals and furnish uniforms. Food and beverage service workers who work full-time often receive paid vacation and sick leave and health insurance, while part-time workers generally do not.

In some large restaurants and hotels, food and beverage service workers belong to unions. The principal unions are the Hotel Employees and Restaurant Employees International Union and the Service Employees International Union.

Related Occupations

Other workers whose jobs involve serving customers and helping them feel at ease and enjoy themselves include flight attendants, butlers, and tour bus drivers.

Sources of Additional Information

Information about job opportunities may be obtained from local employers and local offices of the state employment service.

A guide to careers in restaurants, a list of two- and four-year colleges that have food service programs, and information on scholarships to those programs is available from:

The Educational Foundation of the National Restaurant Association, 250 South Wacker Dr., Suite 1400, Chicago, IL 60606.

For general information on hospitality careers, write to:

Council on Hotel, Restaurant, and Institutional Education, 1200 17th St. NW, Washington, DC 20036-3097.

For general career information and a directory of private career colleges and schools that offer training for bartender and other food and beverage service jobs, write to:

Accrediting Commission of Career Schools and Colleges of Technology, 2101 Wilson Blvd., Suite 302, Arlington, VA 22201.

Computer Programmers

Nature of the Work

Computer programmers write and maintain the detailed instructions—called "programs" or "software"—that list in a logical order the steps that computers must execute to perform their functions. In many large organizations, programmers follow descriptions prepared by systems analysts who have carefully studied the task that the computer system is going to perform. These descriptions list the input required, the steps the computer must follow to process data, and the desired arrangement of the output. Some organizations, particularly smaller ones, do not employ systems analysts. Instead, workers called *programmer-analysts* are responsible for both systems analysis and programming.

Regardless of setting, programmers write specific programs by breaking down each step into a logical series of instructions the computer can follow. They then code these instructions in a conventional programming language, such as C or FORTRAN, or one of the more advanced artificial intelligence or object oriented languages, such as LISP, Prolog, C + +, or Ada.

The transition from a mainframe environment to a primarily PC-based environment has blurred the once rigid distinction between the programmer and the user. Increasingly adept users are taking over many of the tasks previously performed by programmers. For example, the growing use of packaged software, like spreadsheet and data base management software packages, allows users to write simple programs to access data and perform calculations.

Programmers in software development companies may work directly with experts from various fields to create software—either programs designed for specific clients or packaged software for general use—ranging from games and educational software to programs for desktop publishing, financial planning, and spreadsheets. Much of the programming being done today is the preparation of packaged software, one of the most rapidly growing segments of the computer industry.

Despite the prevalence of packaged software, many programmers are involved in updating, repairing, and modifying code for existing programs. When making changes to a section of code, called a "routine," programmers need to make other users aware of the task that the routine is to perform. They do this by inserting comments in the coded instructions so others can understand the program. Programmers using Computer-Aided Software Engineering (CASE) tools can concentrate on writing the unique parts of the program because the tools automate various pieces of the program being built. This also yields more reliable and consistent programs and increases programmers' productivity by eliminating some of the routine steps.

When a program is ready to be tested, programmers run it to ensure that the instructions are correct and will produce the desired information. They prepare sample data that test every part of the program and, after trial runs, review the results to see if any errors were made. If errors do occur, the programmer must make the appropriate changes and recheck the program until it produces the correct results. This is called "debugging" the program.

Finally, programmers working in a mainframe environment prepare instructions for the computer operator who will run the program. They may also contribute to a user's manual for the program.

Programs vary depending upon the type of information to be accessed or generated. For example, the instructions involved in updating financial records are different from those required to duplicate conditions onboard an aircraft for pilots training in a flight simulator. Although simple programs can be written in a few hours, programs that use complex mathematical formulas or many data files may require more than a year of work. In most cases, several programmers work together as a team under a senior programmer's supervision.

Programmers often are grouped into two broad types: Applications programmers and systems programmers. *Applications programmers* usually are oriented toward business, engineering, or science. They write software to handle specific jobs, such as a program used in an inventory control system or one to guide a missile after it has been fired. They also may work alone to revise existing packaged software. *Systems programmers*, on the other hand, maintain the software that controls the operation of an entire computer system. These workers make changes in the sets of instructions that determine how the central processing unit of the system handles the various jobs it has been given and communicates with peripheral equipment, such as terminals, printers, and disk drives. Because of their knowledge of the entire computer system, systems programmers often help applications programmers determine the source of problems that may occur with their programs.

Working Conditions

Programmers generally work in offices in comfortable surroundings. Although they usually work about 40 hours a week, their hours are not always from 9 to 5. Programmers may work longer hours or weekends in order to meet deadlines or fix critical problems that occur during off hours.

Because programmers spend long periods of time in front of a computer monitor typing at a keyboard, they are susceptible to eyestrain, back discomfort, and hand and wrist problems.

Employment

Computer programmers hold about 537,000 jobs. Programmers are employed in most industries, but the largest concentrations are in data processing service organizations, including firms that write and sell software; firms that provide engineering and management services; manufacturers of computer and office equipment; financial institutions; insurance carriers; educational institutions; and government agencies. Applications programmers work for all types of firms, whereas systems programmers usually work for organizations with large computer centers or for firms that manufacture computers or develop software.

A growing number of programmers are employed on a temporary or contract basis. Rather than hiring programmers as permanent employees and then laying them off after a job is completed, employers increasingly are contracting with temporary help agencies, consulting firms, or directly with programmers themselves. A marketing firm, for example, may only require the services of several programmers to write and "debug" the software necessary to get a new database management system running. Such jobs may last from several months to a year or longer.

Training, Other Qualifications, and Advancement

There are no universal training requirements for programmers because employers' needs are so varied. Computer applications have become so widespread that computer programming is taught at most public and private vocational schools, community and junior colleges, and universities. However, the levels of education and quality of training that employers seek have been rising due to the growth in the number of qualified applicants and the increasing complexity of some programming tasks. Although some programmers obtain two-year degrees or certificates, bachelor's degrees are now commonly required. In the absence of a degree, substantial specialized experience or expertise may be needed.

The majority of programmers hold a four-year degree. Of these, some hold a B.A. or B.S. in computer science or information systems while others have taken special courses in computer programming to supplement their study in fields such as accounting, inventory control, or other business areas. College graduates who are interested in changing careers or developing an area of expertise may return to a junior college or technical school for more training.

Employers using computers for scientific or engineering applications prefer college graduates who have degrees in computer or information science, mathematics, engineering, or the physical sciences. Graduate degrees are required for some jobs. Employers who use computers for business applications prefer to hire people who have had college courses in management information systems (MIS) and business, and who possess strong programming skills. Knowledge of FORTRAN, COBOL, C, Fourth Generation Languages (4GL), CASE tools, systems programming, C++, Smalltalk, and other object-oriented programming languages is highly desirable. General business skills and experience related to the operations of the firm are preferred by employers as well.

Most systems programmers hold a four-year degree in computer science. Extensive knowledge of a variety of operating systems is essential. This includes being able to configure the operating system to work with different types of hardware, and adapting the operating system to best meet the needs of the particular organization. They also must be able to work with database systems such as DB2, Oracle, or Sybase, for example.

The Institute for Certification of Computing Professionals confers the designation Certified Computing Professional (CCP) to those who have at least four years of experience or two years of experience and a college degree. To qualify, individuals must pass a core examination plus exams in two specialty areas, or an exam in one specialty area and two computing languages. Those with

121

little or no experience may be tested for certification as an Associate Computer Professional (ACP). Certification is not mandatory, but it may give a job seeker a competitive advantage.

When hiring programmers, employers look for people with the necessary programming skills who can think logically and pay close attention to detail. The job calls for patience, persistence, and the ability to work on exacting analytical work, especially under pressure. Ingenuity and imagination are also particularly important when programmers design solutions and test their work for potential failures. Increasingly, interpersonal skills are important as programmers are expected to work in teams and interact directly with users. The ability to work with abstract concepts and do technical analysis is especially important for systems programmers because they work with the software that controls the computer's operation.

Beginning programmers may spend their first weeks on the job attending training classes, since each business has its own development methodology, processes, and tools. After this initial instruction, they may work alone on simple assignments or on a team with more experienced programmers. Either way, they generally must spend at least several months working under close supervision. Because of rapidly changing technology, programmers must continuously update their training by taking courses sponsored by their employer or software vendors.

For skilled workers, the prospects for advancement are good. In large organizations, they may be promoted to lead programmer and given supervisory responsibilities. Some applications programmers may move into systems programming after they gain experience and take courses in systems software. With general business experience, both applications programmers and systems programmers may become systems analysts or be promoted to a managerial position. Other programmers, with specialized knowledge and experience with a language or operating system, may work in research and development areas such as multimedia or Internet technology. As employers increasingly contract out programming jobs, more opportunities should arise for experienced programmers with expertise in a specific area to work as consultants.

Job Outlook

Employment of programmers is expected to grow about as fast as the average for all occupations through the year 2005. Employment is not expected to grow as rapidly as in the past as improved software and programming techniques continue to simplify programming tasks. In addition, greater use of packaged software—such as word processing and spreadsheet packages—should continue to moderate the growth in demand for applications programmers. As the level of technological innovation and sophistication increases, users will be able to design, write, and implement more of their own programs to meet their changing needs.

Although the proportion of programmers leaving the occupation each year is smaller than that of most occupations, most of the job openings for programmers will result from replacement needs. The majority of programmers who leave transfer to other occupations, such as manager or systems analyst. Jobs for both systems and applications programmers, however, should remain particularly plentiful in data processing service firms, software houses, and computer consulting businesses. These types of establishments remain part of one of the fastest growing industries—computer and data processing services. As companies look to control costs, those in need of programming services should look to this industry to meet these needs.

As computer usage expands, however, the demand for skilled programmers will increase as organizations seek new applications for computers and improvements to the software already in use. Employers are increasingly interested in programmers who can combine areas of technical expertise or who are adaptable and able to learn and incorporate new skills. One area of progress will be data communications. Networking computers so they can communicate with each other is necessary to achieve the greater efficiency that organizations require to remain competitive. Object-oriented languages will increasingly be used in the years ahead, further enhancing the productivity of programmers. Programmers will be creating and maintaining expert systems and embedding these technologies in more and more products.

The number and quality of applicants for programmer jobs have increased, so employers have become more selective. Graduates of two-year programs in data processing, and people with less than a two-year degree or its equivalent in work experience, are facing especially strong competition for programming jobs. Competition for entry-level positions even affects applicants with a bachelor's degree. Many observers expect opportunities for people without college degrees to diminish in coming years as programming tasks become more complex and more sophisticated skills and experience are demanded by employers. Prospects should be good for college graduates with knowledge of a variety of programming languages, particularly C + + and other object-oriented languages, as well as newer languages that apply to computer networking, data base management, and artificial intelligence. In order to remain competitive, college graduates should keep up to date with the latest skills and technologies.

Many employers prefer to hire applicants with previous experience in the field. Firms also desire programmers who develop a technical specialization in areas such as client/server programming, multimedia technology, graphic user interface, or fourth- and fifth-generation programming tools. Therefore, people who want to become programmers can enhance their chances by combining work experience with the appropriate formal training. Students should try to gain experience by participating in a college work-study program, or undertaking an internship. Students also can greatly improve their employment prospects by taking courses such as accounting, management, engineering, or science—allied fields in which applications programmers are in demand. With the expansion of client/server environments, employers will continue to look for programmers with strong technical skills, as well as good interpersonal and business skills.

Earnings

Median earnings of programmers who worked full-time were about $38,400 a year. The middle 50 percent earned between $30,000 and $49,200 a year. The lowest 10 percent earned less than $22,000, and the highest 10 percent earned more than $60,600.

According to Robert Half International, Inc., starting salaries in large establishments ranged from $29,500 to $36,500 for programmers; $36,000 to $47,000 for programmer analysts; and $44,000 to $54,000 for systems programmers. Starting salaries in small establishments ranged from $25,000 to $34,000 for programmers and from $30,000 to $40,000 for programmer analysts.

Programmers working in the West and Northeast earned somewhat more than those working in the South and Midwest. On average, systems programmers earn more than applications programmers.

In the federal government, the entrance salary for programmers with a college degree or qualifying experience was about $18,700 a year; for those with a superior academic record, $23,200.

Related Occupations

Programmers must pay great attention to detail as they write and debug programs. Other professional workers who must be detail-oriented include statisticians, engineers, financial analysts, accountants, auditors, actuaries, and operations research analysts.

Sources of Additional Information

State employment service offices can provide information about job openings for computer programmers. Also check with your city's chamber of commerce for information on the area's largest employers.

For information about certification as a computing professional, contact:

> Institute for the Certification of Computing Professionals, 2200 East Devon Ave., Suite 268, Des Plaines, IL 60018.

Further information about computer careers is available from:

> The Association for Computing Machinery, 1515 Broadway, New York, NY 10036.

123

Other Sources of Career Help and Information

Career Counselors

If you have access to a career counselor, consider yourself fortunate and set up an appointment. A good career counselor can help you in many ways, including in planning your education and training. Many schools provide career counseling, and there are many good career counselors in community organizations and in private practice. To locate them, look in the *Yellow Pages* of the phone book. Keep in mind, however, that just because a person says he or she does career counseling does not mean he or she is good at it. And if a counselor won't tell you his or her fees up front, it's probably best to stay away.

Career Tests

There are two types of career-related tests you are likely to use. The first includes career interest tests. There are a variety of them available from several publishers. They all do the same basic thing: They ask you questions to help you identify groups of jobs that interest you. Some of the better-known interest tests include the *Self-Directed Search (SDS)*; the *Career Exploration Inventory (CEI)*; the *Career Decision Making System (CDM)*; and the *Guide for Occupational Exploration Inventory*. Any of these tests can be helpful in identifying careers you want to consider more carefully.

The other type of career test is one that measures your abilities to do various jobs. These tests may measure clerical skills, math abilities, eye-hand coordination, and other job-related skills. Such tests can provide you with helpful information on which types of jobs you are best suited for, although they will *not* tell you if you will enjoy those jobs.

There are other kinds of tests—such as personality and learning style tests—that can provide useful information. Remember, though, that any test has limitations. A test can only provide additional information to help you make decisions. It can't decide what to do for you.

More Career Information

At the end of this book is a listing of career references. I have also listed a few of the most important sources of career information here. These books will be available at a good library or career counselor's office.

I have already recommended that you start your search for career information with the job descriptions in the *Occupational Outlook Handbook* or *America's Top 300 Jobs*. These books provide excellent descriptions for hundreds of major jobs that cover about 85 percent of the U.S. workforce. However, while the *OOH* is an excellent source of information, it does have limitations. For one thing, it describes only major jobs, such as "secretaries," but not the more specialized jobs that might appeal to you.

Other books provide descriptions or cross-referencing to the many more specialized jobs. Following is a list of those I think are most helpful.

▼ *The Complete Guide for Occupational Exploration (CGOE)*. Lists more than 12,000 job titles in a format that makes it easy to use for exploring career alternatives based on current skills. Jobs with similar characteristics are grouped together, and each grouping includes details on skills required, nature of work, and other information. The *CGOE* also cross-references to other standard reference sources for additional information.

▼ *The Enhanced Guide for Occupational Exploration (EGOE)*. Uses the same organizational structure as the *CGOE* and includes brief descriptions of about 2,800 jobs. Useful for career exploration, identifying skills used in previous jobs, researching new job targets, and preparing for interviews.

▼ *Dictionary of Occupational Titles (DOT)*. Provides descriptions for more than 12,000 jobs, covering virtually all jobs in the U.S. economy. While not easy to use, this is the only book of its kind. It can be used to identify jobs in different fields that use skills similar to those you have acquired in past jobs and to identify key skills to emphasize in interviews. It provides brief descriptions for each job and additional coded information.

▼ *Young Person's Occupational Outlook Handbook*. Provides interesting and up-to-date information on 250 of the most important jobs in our workforce in an entertaining, easy-to-use format.

▼ *Career Guide to America's Top Industries*. Provides trends and other information on more than 40 major industries and summary data on many others. Excellent for getting information on an industry prior to an interview. Includes details on employment projections, advancement opportunities, major trends, and a complete narrative description of each industry.

The Career Objective Worksheet

This section reviews different ways to receive career training or education. But before considering those options, you should do two things:

▼ Clearly state what sort of job you want.

▼ Know the kinds of skills and experiences needed to do well in that job.

Even if you change your job objective later, you should decide on at least a temporary objective now. To help you with this, complete the following worksheet, referring to earlier chapters of this book for the information. Feel free to make copies of this worksheet if you are considering several job options.

1. Name the type of job you want (use your own words).

    _____

    _____

    _____

    _____

2. Name the specific occupational category and job title (or as close to a specific title as possible).

    _____

    _____

    _____

    _____

3. List your adaptive skills that this job requires. (Refer to The Adaptive Skills Checklist in Chapter 2.)

    _____

    _____

    _____

    _____

    _____

4. Review the Transferable Skills Checklist in Chapter 2. List your transferable skills required by this job. Circle the five most important ones.

    _____

    _____

    _____

    _____

    _____

    _____

5. List your specific job-content skills or knowledge that directly relates to this particular job.(Name as many as possible, referring to your job content skills listed in Chapter 2.)

_____   _____

_____   _____

_____   _____

_____   _____

_____   _____

6. Describe any special training or education you have that directly supports your doing this job well.

_____

_____

_____

_____

_____

7. List all special tools or equipment you can operate that relate to doing this job well.

_____

_____

_____

_____

_____

8. Describe any specific work experiences that relate to your doing this job well (similar duties, tasks, responsibilities, etc.).

_____

_____

_____

_____

_____

9. Describe anything else that supports your doing this job well.

_____

_____

_____

_____

10. Write a statement that summarizes why you want this job. Possible factors to include are how it suits your lifestyle, what rewards you expect to receive, and how it meets your needs.

_____

_____

_____

_____

11. Write down any barriers you know of that you will need to overcome in order to enter this job (for example, the need for additional training or education.)

_____

_____

_____

_____

Unless you can answer all these items thoroughly, you are not ready to conduct an effective job search. If necessary, seek help from other sources, but do settle on a career objective before you embark on your actual job search.

Sources of Career Training and Education

Now that you have had a chance to review sources of information on jobs that interest you, you should consider the training and educational requirements for those jobs. If you don't already have the necessary training or education, now is the time to consider how you might get it. Generally, the more education or training you have, the more you are likely to be paid. So it is probably worth the extra time and money it takes to qualify yourself for a job in which your interest is high. But pay is only one consideration in making career decisions. Finding a job you enjoy is also important.

How Much Training and Education Do You Need?

Some jobs will be available to you only if you have the training or education required. Like a hobby or sport, every job involves knowledge and skills that you must learn. For example, it doesn't make sense to aim for a career as a veterinarian unless you do well in school, are interested in science, and are willing to put seven years or more of hard work into an educational program.

Think about your attitude toward continuing or going back to school. How long are you willing to stay in school? Are you willing to take training that lasts six months? What about training that lasts two to four years? Is college a possibility? Are you willing to study after college for another year or more? Some occupations, such as veterinary science, require years of formal education beyond college.

The Cost of Education and Training

Education or training can be costly. But remember that earnings often increase enough to pay for these costs quickly. For example, average annual earnings for a person with a two-year associate degree are $6,000 more than average earnings for a high school graduate. And those with a four-year college degree earn an average of $14,000 a year more.

Don't let the cost of education or training keep you from considering occupations that interest you. There are many sources of financial aid available and many ways to finance the education you want. The most important thing is to select the *right* career for you, then find a way to prepare for that career.

Many schools will help you find financial aid. Many adults also work full- or part-time while going to school. This approach may take longer than a traditional approach to education, but it also allows you to pay your own way.

Within most of the career clusters, you will find occupations with different levels of training. The training to become a veterinarian is much more expensive than that for a medical technologist, yet both are health occupations. So keep your options open as you explore career alternatives and do not eliminate any because you "can't afford" the needed education or training.

Training and Education Options

There many ways to get the education and training you need for the career you want. The path you choose depends on the amount of time, effort, and money you're willing to invest. Read on for a summary of each of these options:

▼   On-the-job training

▼   Apprenticeship programs that combine on-the-job training with classroom instruction

129

▼ Vocational and technical schools that train you to enter a specific job, with programs lasting from several months to a year or more

▼ Two-year associate degree programs

▼ Four-year college degrees

▼ Degrees beyond a bachelor's

▼ Training and work experience in the armed forces

▼ Informal training

On-the-Job Training

All jobs require at least some on-the-job training. Many jobs do not require any formal education or training and are learned on the job. If you have good basic skills, jobs such as cashier and some factory assembly jobs can be learned in a just a few hours or days. These jobs are learned by helping and observing more experienced workers and working under their supervision.

More complex jobs can require months of on-the-job training and even some formal training. For example, power truck operators require classroom instruction as well as supervised, on-the-job experience. For some occupations, on-the-job training continues for several years. Air traffic controllers, for example, take a 16-week course and must complete independent study courses. They also must work for two or three years under the supervision of an experienced controller before being considered fully qualified.

Employers often will train employees with good basic skills to handle specialized jobs such as desktop publishing, computer graphic design, or warehouse automation because there are shortages of people with these skills.

Apprenticeship Programs

An apprenticeship is a method of learning a trade that combines on-the-job training with classroom instruction. Apprenticeship programs last from one to six years. Most are sponsored by employers, government programs, and labor unions. When you have completed an apprenticeship, you are formally recognized as being fully qualified in your trade.

As an apprentice, you are taught by experienced workers. You learn by helping them and working under their supervision. Your training covers all aspects of the trade. For example, apprentice mechanics learn not only how to repair engines but also how to diagnose engine problems and how to take care of their tools. They also attend classes or complete home-study assignments on topics such as shop safety practices and customer relations.

People learn to become carpenters, bricklayers, electricians, chefs, brick masons, and other trade professionals through formal apprenticeship programs.

Vocational and Technical Schools

There are excellent job-training programs available at both the high school and postsecondary levels.

High School Programs

Most high schools provide a general education that prepares graduates to go on to college. In addition, many have specialized programs that prepare students for direct entry into jobs following graduation. Larger school districts often pool their resources and offer a variety of job-related programs at a vocational or technical high school.

Some of the job-related courses can be basic, such as keyboarding or business principles. These can be taken as electives along with general education courses. More specialized programs are often available and provide many more hours of instruction. Examples include building trades, automotive technology, health technology, marketing and sales, agriculture, general business, printing, drafting, desktop publishing, computer repair, accounting, appliance repair, and secretarial.

Depending on the quality of these programs, they can prepare graduates for immediate entry into jobs. Many high school vocational programs have high success rates, with many of their graduates finding good-paying jobs in areas that interest them. High school students should definitely consider vocational programs if one or more is of interest. These programs also can prepare students to go on to college in a related interest area.

Postsecondary Vocational and Technical Schools

Most communities have a variety of schools that provide formal training to high school graduates and adults on job-related topics. Shorter programs (that do not result in a two-year associate degree) are available to prepare students for entry into an enormous variety of occupations. Programs may last several weeks up to two years. Such programs are offered at trade schools, technical institutes, business schools, and correspondence or home-study schools.

Some of the programs offered by these schools include electronics, commercial aircraft piloting, cosmetology or barbering, business and office procedures, computer operating and programming, medical technology, auto mechanics, locksmithing, truck driving, and real estate sales.

Most of these programs do not provide general education courses such as history, English, or math. Instead, they focus on skills directly related to doing a particular job. In business school, for example, you would learn word-processing and spreadsheet programs, basic accounting principles, and how to write correspondence. In health occupation training programs, you would learn a variety of medical procedures and how to operate medical equipment. Mechanics and repairers take classes in blueprint reading and shop math. Medical technicians take classes in basic chemistry, human physiology, and medical record keeping.

In addition to classroom learning, these schools often provide practical experience using skills in an actual job. This is done under the close supervision of an instructor. For example, cosmetology students practice their skills on one another and on people who come to the school to have their hair done. Computer repair technicians repair real computers. Medical technologists simulate on-the-job tasks in a realistic job setting such as a medical office. Some schools also arrange for students to work in real job settings as part of their educational experience.

Students completing a vocational or technical program receive a certificate of achievement. They are generally ready to begin work when they complete the program, although most employers will provide on-the-job training as well. Some states require students to take a licensing exam for some occupations before they begin working.

Some Occupations Typically Requiring Postsecondary Training

▼ Secretaries, including medical and legal

▼ Licensed practical nurses

▼ Hairdressers, hair stylers, and cosmetologists

▼ Data entry keyers

▼ Welders

▼ Drafters

▼ Real estate sales agents

▼ Emergency medical technicians

▼ Travel agents

▼ Stenographers

▼ Aircraft mechanics

▼ Surveyors

▼ Data processing equipment repairers

▼ Electronics equipment repairers

▼ Barbers

▼ Surgical technologists

▼ Broadcast technicians

▼ Manicurists

▼ Telephone equipment installers and repairers

▼ Electronic home entertainment equipment repairers

▼ Dancers and choreographers

While almost all vocational and technical schools charge fees, there are differences among them. Public institutions are funded by state or local governments. Private schools are operated by not-for-profit organizations or, more often, by for-profit businesses. While you should know the difference before you enroll, one is not necessarily better than the other.

For example, private schools often are required to meet certain standards and are supervised by the state government. And, unlike public schools, private schools must meet certain goals for their students getting and keeping jobs related to their training. Some for-profit career schools also have more modern equipment and higher-quality curricula than publicly funded institutions.

You should carefully evaluate any program you consider. Some schools use high-pressure sales techniques to get you to enroll in their programs. Be careful, because you will be responsible for paying for any program you enroll in, and the fees can be substantial. Financial aid offers can make some programs seem very attractive, but don't sign anything if you feel under pressure to do so. Insist on going home and thinking things over first.

Ask about the accreditation of any program you are considering. Accreditation by a national or regional association is important; it means the association requires the program to meet a variety of standards. Get details of the accreditation standards that are required. Schools that are accredited are proud of this and will be happy to give you the information you want. Also ask for information on the placement rates of previous graduates. Programs with good results will be happy to share the information. Schools that provide meaningful help in getting a job after graduation are worth more than those that do not. Ask about their job-finding programs, and consider this in your decision.

Community and Junior Colleges

Many areas have community colleges or junior colleges. These schools provide career-oriented programs lasting two years or less as well as courses that can be transferred to a four-year college or university program. You can earn a two-year associate degree in such colleges, but they are also a good source of shorter vocational programs or courses on specific job-related topics.

Two-Year Associate Degrees

Many local colleges allow you to earn an associate degree. Most such degrees are job-related and take from one to three years to complete. These degrees can be earned from private and public colleges, technical schools, and business colleges.

The associate degree prepares you to enter a specific career. The requirements for an associate degree are more demanding than

those for a technical school. They often include courses in advanced mathematics, science, and applied theory as well as job-related courses.

Four-Year Colleges and Universities

These schools require classes in a variety of subjects such as English, psychology, history, and math. Graduates of these schools earn a bachelor's degree.

You can select a *major* and take several courses in a particular subject area such as art, music, chemistry, engineering, or business. Some of these majors help prepare you for work in a particular profession, such as teaching or accounting, while others provide you with a general education that will help you in a variety of careers.

Jobs held by college graduates are quite varied. Many jobs require a college degree for entry. In many other occupations, having a four-year college degree gives you a competitive advantage over those without such a degree.

C.L.E.P./C.P.E. Tests

The College Level Exam Program (or C.L.E.P.) grants college credit through examination for knowledge students have gained on the job, through life experience, or in correspondence courses. The general exam is multiple choice, covering English composition, humanities, mathematics, natural sciences, and social sciences/history. A subject exam measures overall competence in a specific subject. The College Proficiency Exam (or C.P.E.) is similar to C.L.E.P. but provides credit specifically in areas of nursing sciences, foreign language, and professional education.

These exams are an excellent way to test out of programs and advance more rapidly toward a degree than is otherwise possible. You prepare your own schedule. Aids for preparation are available. Most universities, colleges, and community colleges can provide you with information about these programs.

Degrees Beyond the Bachelor's

Some occupations require more than a four-year bachelor's degree. A master's degree requires one or two years of college beyond a bachelor's. A doctoral degree requires one or more years beyond the master's degree. And professional degrees require two or more years beyond the bachelor's degree: A physician, for example, will require as many as six years beyond the bachelor's.

Some Jobs Typically Requiring at Least an Associate Degree

▼ Registered nurses

▼ Engineering technologists

▼ Electrical and electronic technologists, health technologists

▼ Science and math technicians

▼ Radiologic technicians

▼ Dental hygienists

▼ Paralegals

▼ Medical records technicians

▼ Legal assistants

▼ Respiratory therapists

▼ Psychiatric technicians

▼ Veterinary technologists

▼ Cardiology technologists

▼ Nuclear medicine technologists

133

Some Occupations at the Various Degree Levels

▼ **Professional degree:** Lawyers; Physicians; Clergy; Dentists; Veterinarians; Chiropractors; Optometrists; Podiatrists

▼ **Doctoral degree:** College and university faculty; Biological scientists; Medical scientists; Physicists and astronomers; Mathematicians; Life scientists

▼ **Master's degree:** Teachers and instructors; Management analysts; Counselors; Professional librarians; Psychologists; Speech-language pathologists; Operations research analysts; Urban and regional planners; Curators, archivists, museum technicians, and restorers

Major Areas of Study

⸍ ⸍ Agriculture and Natural Resources

⸍ ⸍ Art

⸍ ⸍ Biological Science

⸍ ⸍ Business and Management

▼ Chemistry

⸍ ⸍ Communications

⸍ ⸍ Computer and Information Science

⸍ ⸍ Economics

⸍ ⸍ Education

⸍ ⸍ Engineering

⸍ ⸍ History

⸍ ⸍ Home Economics

⸍ ⸍ Physical Education

⸍ ⸍ Political Science

⸍ ⸍ Psychology

⸍ ⸍ Sociology

The Armed Forces

The various branches of the armed forces provide many opportunities for long-term careers. People train in the military for many of the same occupations available outside the military. They learn to be cooks, clerks, secretaries, nurses, carpenters, mechanics, newspaper reporters, photographers, meteorologists, and air traffic controllers, to name just a few.

While in the service, you can learn job skills and gain work experience. When you complete your tour of duty, these skills and experiences can be used to qualify for civilian jobs. *America's Top Military Careers* (published by JIST Works) and many other books provide details about careers for which training is available and which branches of service provide that training.

You also can participate in various armed forces scholarship or tuition aid programs that pay for college or technical training after you finish active duty. Some college students finance their education by participating in the Reserve Officer Training Corps (ROTC) while they go to college. After they graduate, they serve in the armed forces for several years.

Other Adult Education Programs

Most communities have a variety of programs that offer excellent low-cost training services that are often overlooked. For example, some public and vocational high schools offer continuing education courses in the evening on topics such as G.E.D. preparation, photography, auto repair, and word processing. Churches, libraries, museums, and other community-based organizations may offer similar programs.

The cost of such programs is often very low. Typically, no formal credit is given, but these programs often are excellent sources of useful information that can help you develop new job skills or leisure activities. Check local newspapers and bulletins for announcements, or call the local public school system and other likely organizations for information.

Educational Considerations Worksheet

Once you are ready to start taking serious steps toward acquiring more education or training, you will have a lot of information to sort through. Having decided what kind of job you need the training for, and why you want it, the next step is to settle on the best way to get that training.

Use the chart that follows to organize information about the educational programs you are considering and to compare them. Write the names of the schools in the left-hand column. Across the top, write the 10 criteria that are most important to you (for example, cost, facilities, job placement rate). Put a check in the appropriate box for each of your criteria that the programs meet.

It's been said before, but it's worth repeating: *Don't be discouraged by obstacles to further education.* There are ways to get financial aid, although you might have to be persistent in finding them. And there are ways to juggle work schedules, family, and other responsibilities. Weigh short-term sacrifices against the benefits of long-term goals. Remember that if something is really important to you, chances are good that it's worth the time and work it takes to achieve it. An excellent resource for learning more about going back to school, financial aid, and adult-friendly programs is *Back to School: A College Guide for Adults*, by LaVerne Ludden (Indianapolis: JIST Works).

If you are having trouble making up your mind about whether to seek further training or education, the next chapter offers some help in making decisions.

Criteria of Programs Under Consideration Worksheet

My Criteria

School or Program							

Making Good Decisions About Your Career and Your Life

You make decisions each day, although some are more important than others. For example, deciding what to have for breakfast is not a terribly important decision and is probably not worth much of your attention. But more important decisions are worth more of your time.

This chapter will teach you methods to use for making important decisions. Many people make even the most important decisions without much planning, and this can be a big mistake. While this chapter will concentrate on career-related decisions, the methods you will learn here can be used to make any important decision.

First Things First: Organize

Let's say you're thinking about going to school (or going back to school). You've looked into a few programs and gotten details on cost, length of the program, and entrance requirements. Some of this information is scribbled on scraps of paper you think you left in a coat hanging in the hall closet; some is in a notebook either in the car or on the desk upstairs; and the rest is in your head—you didn't write it down because you figured you would remember it.

Important decisions need more attention than this. People who make important decisions in such a disorganized way often regret their decisions. You already have an advantage over most people. By doing the activities in this book, you have already gathered and organized much of the information you need to make good career and life decisions.

If you are making a decision that involves a major lifestyle issue with many details to consider, begin by making a list of the information you'll need and how to obtain it.

This helps you avoid overlooking things that may make the difference between choosing one option or another.

The Information-Gathering Worksheet

This worksheet will help you take the first step in making an important decision. It begins by asking you to write down the decision you are considering. For example, you might write, "Should I get more education?" Or, "What sort of career should I consider?"

The "What I need to know" column asks you to identify things you need to find out in order to make this decision. If you were considering more education, some of the things you might write in this column are these:

▼ What schools provide the kind of training or education I want?

▼ How much will it cost?

▼ Is financial aid available?

Once you have completed the first column, go back and complete the column titled, "Where or how to get information." Make notes here of how you can get the information you need. You can include books or other resources, people you need to talk to, appointments to make, and other details.

The third column, titled "Follow-up and notes," will help you organize your follow-up. Use it to write notes on when to contact someone, information you get as you learn more, and other notes.

Making the Decision

Once you have gathered and organized the information you need to make a decision, you can take the next step. Most of the time, you will already have a good idea of what you want to do. So what you need to do now is make sure this is the decision you really want to make.

Decision you are trying to make:

What I need to know	Where or how to get information	Follow-up and notes

Scenario #1:

You are driving down a mountain road, alongside a steep drop-off. Suddenly, you see a car speeding toward you, out of control. There is no time to thoroughly analyze all the advantages and disadvantages of the choices available to you. You have to make a snap decision: stay on the road or veer off the cliff. The action you take may save your life. In other words, at the heart of a snap decision you make in a life-and-death situation is what you sense to be in your best interests.

Scenario #2:

You're standing by the water cooler at work when you see your boss heading toward you. You know she is going to ask you about the project that should be done by now. It isn't—because your co-worker, having been up all night with a sick child, came in late, and you couldn't complete it without her. Your boss is interested in results, not excuses. You have to make a snap decision: tell her the real reason the project was delayed or give an excuse that saves your co-worker but leaves you open for criticism. In this case, there is no life-or-death issue. But the action you take, with a split second to decide, will say a lot about your values.

Here are two scenarios of how you might make a typical decision. They will help you see how different types of decisions are made.

In both of these scenarios, you are forced to make quick decisions. Quick decisions can turn out well, and the next section will review these kinds of decisions. But any decision can also turn out badly. For most decisions you have to make, you will have time for more preparation than in these examples. Let's look more closely at the process of making decisions.

Making Use of Snap Decisions

A snap decision is the initial feeling you have about a course of action before you stop to think it through. Over the course of human evolution, people have come to depend more on logic and less on instinct or intuition. But when you consider how complex the interaction is between our thoughts and our emotions, it is easy to see that both reason and intuition have a role to play in the choices we make.

Some people base their decisions solely on reason; they ignore their intuition and always do the "logical" thing. Too often, the result is that they don't feel good about their decision. Other people typically throw logic out the window and decide impulsively on things that, later, just don't make sense. Learning to make use of both reason and intuition will help you make better decisions.

Some Points Regarding Snap Decisions

Here are some things to consider about snap or intuitive decisions.

▼ Making quick decisions can be important for our survival.

▼ They are sometimes right and sometimes wrong.

▼ We nearly always make an initial decision about something, even if the situation doesn't require one.

▼ We often change our snap decisions when we have the time to think more about a choice we're facing.

▼ We can use our snap decisions as one basis for making good choices.

Why Decision Making Creates Anxiety

If you are like most people, you feel anxious when you are faced with an important decision. This anxiety does not mean you can't make up your mind. It means you don't know how to be sure that the choice you are leaning toward is the right one. So you need a reliable way to test your intuition. If you can test it, you will know better why it is or is not the best choice.

There is such a test. The technique is simple, and you can try it out right now.

Testing a Snap Decision

Think of a decision you're trying to make. It can be anything, major or minor. Now ask yourself, "What is my snap decision on this?" Write the answer on the first two lines that follow.

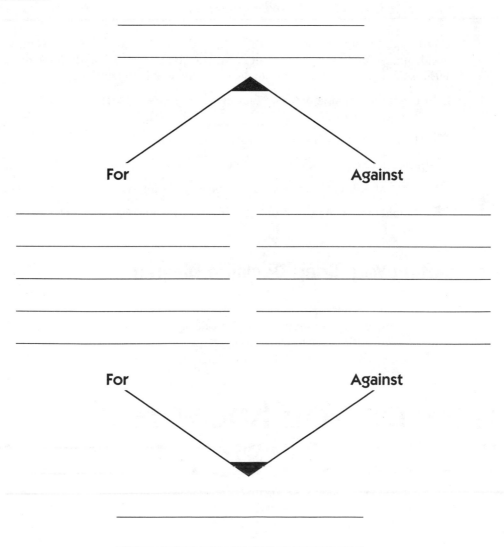

Next, on the "For" side of the diagram, write any advantages that favor your snap decision. Think quickly—this is a time for brainstorming.

Now move to the "Against" side, and make a list of any disadvantages that come to mind.

Notice how your diagram resembles a weight scale. This gives you an immediate feel for which side is "tipping the scale."

A Second Look at the Advantages

Now, carefully consider each item on the "For" side. Put a check beside those that seem important. You may end up with check marks beside all of them, which is fine. Or you may find that some of the advantages you listed don't matter as much as they seemed to at first. Feel free to jot down notes about each item you listed, explaining why it remains important or why it doesn't.

A Second Look at the Disadvantages

Go through the same process on the "Against" side. You may find that some of the disadvantages are not as important as others. You may also find that one disadvantage is serious enough to make your snap decision impossible to feel good about.

Before you draw that conclusion, however, ask yourself these questions:

▼ Is there anything I can do about this disadvantage?

▼ Do I have all the information I need about it?

▼ Am I afraid that this *might* be a problem, or do I know in fact that it *will* be?

▼ Would discussing this problem with someone make a difference?

Completing Your Snap Decision Diagram

Now go back to your snap decision diagram. At the bottom of the diamond, where the two lines come to a point, write down the decision that feels good *right now*. Is it the same as your initial decision?

How Do You Know You've Reached the Right Decision?

You can *never* be sure you are making the right decision. Even if you are wonderfully well-organized and construct admirable diagrams, there are no guarantees that every decision you make will work out well.

We can't look into the future to know how a decision will turn out. A good decision requires you to make the best choice with the information you have *now*.

For important decisions, it's worth the effort to be as thorough as possible in gathering information and considering all the options. You may end up with an entire notebook full of diamond diagrams and scribbles. But when you reach the "right" decision, you'll know it. You might feel stressful about what you have decided to do (go back to school, change jobs, take flying lessons, whatever), but it is a better feeling than worrying about which decision to make.

Taking the Plunge

Another way to tell that you believe in the decision you have reached is that you feel ready to take action. If you still feel anxious and you are not ready to act, go back to your diagrams. Look for the missing elements. Consider what information you have overlooked, or those things that concern you most.

Be Aware of How Your Decisions Affect Others

Remember to consider how your actions affect people around you. Also be aware that parents, spouses, children, friends, co-workers, and others influence both your logic and your intuition—the way you think and the way you feel. It is your decision to make, but you must consider its impact on others.

More Tips for Effective Decision-Making Diagrams

Be as open and honest in your diagrams as you would be in a diary. Consider the following factors in making your decision:

▼ Fear of making a change

▼ Feeling pressured to make a change

▼ Worry about what others think of you

▼ Fears of "not being good enough"

If these or similar issues turn up, ask yourself, "What can I do about it?"

As you practice balancing intuition with logic, you will gain confidence in your ability to make decisions that make sense and feel right. So go ahead and practice now using blank sheets of paper to make as many diagrams as you want.

More Practice for Making Decisions

1. Think of a decision that has been on your mind recently. In the space below, describe the situation and why it has been difficult to make a decision. Understand that, sometimes, *not* making a decision really *is* a decision.

   _____

   _____

   _____

   _____

   _____

2. Use the decision-making diagram shown earlier to explore the advantages and disadvantages of the decision you are having trouble making. You'll need blank sheets of paper for your practice exercises. First, draw just the top half of the diagram on your paper, writing your snap decision at the top.

   Now list all the items you can think of on the "For" side and all you can think of on the "Against" side. Go through each list quickly, checking the most important items. Then go through each of the items more carefully, jotting down notes about each if you wish. Are there any items that stand out as most important?

   Finally, draw the rest of the diagram, writing at the bottom the decision that feels like the right one. Compare it to what you wrote at the top of the diagram.

Improving your decision-making skills is valuable in whatever career path you choose and throughout your life. As with any skill, the more you practice decision making, the more natural it becomes.

And when you are as sure as you can be about the choice you have made, don't hold back. Go for it!

Special Tips for Special People

If you are reading this book, you probably have a definite goal: to discover the work best suited to your skills, interests, values, and lifestyle. This book was designed to help readers do that, regardless of age, race, gender, abilities, or limitations. Here are tips for situations some people face in the job market.

Minorities

Discrimination on the basis of minority status in this country is illegal and immoral. Employers want to hire people who can perform well. If you possess those qualifications, your race, religion, gender, or nationality shouldn't matter. Conduct your job search as if you expect to be treated according to your merits.

People with Disabilities

A disability matters only if it affects your performance in the job you want to do. Be realistic about your abilities, but don't assume that employers won't be interested in you if you have a disability. Like any other job seeker, you should emphasize what you *can do* and what you want to do. Everyone has disabilities—whether visible or not—and everyone has areas of strength as well.

Homemakers and Others Reentering the Workforce

If you are a homemaker preparing to enter or reenter the paid workforce, you are in good company. More than 50 percent of American women currently work outside the home, and the number continues to rise. Women work for the same reasons men do: to support themselves and their families. They also want work that gives them satisfaction and a sense of accomplishment. But women are still far more likely than men to take extended periods off work or to leave the workforce altogether to raise young children or run a household.

Key Idea

Turn any job you take into an opportunity to get experience and earn a good reference for the future.

Reentering the paid workforce after a long absence can be a hard adjustment. This is especially true when a return to work is made necessary by a stressful event such as divorce, death of a spouse, or pressing financial need. When you have to get a job as quickly as possible, it's tempting to take the first thing that comes along. But that can become a trap of low wages and little chance for promotion.

There are ways to avoid falling into that trap. If you must take a stopgap job for the sake of a paycheck, commit yourself to high standards just as you would for your ideal job. Meanwhile, continue to develop long-term objectives, and plan a strategy to obtain the kind of work you really want.

Remember that employers are especially interested in adaptive and transferable skills (review Chapter 2). Your experiences managing a household and/or raising children have helped you develop a wide range of skills you might tend to overlook or undervalue. A homemaker's skills might include budgeting, coordinating schedules and activities, planning events, negotiating contracts, organizing, record keeping, and so on. Opposite is an example of a resume for a woman who had always been a homemaker. It's an eye-opener!

Check the local public library for books about home-based work you can do to supplement your income. Keep in mind, too, that people are changing or entering new careers at all different ages. Your willingness to work hard and learn as much as possible will go a long way toward compensating for a late start or lack of experience in the career field you have chosen.

Students

If you are interested in part-time work while you're in school, there is no reason you have to settle for "just anything." Even if you're not sure of your career objectives yet, part-time work can be a good way to explore possibilities for the future. Volunteering, if you can do without the wages, is another way to do this. You might also be able to take advantage of work-study programs at your school that can help you begin developing skills in the career field that interests you.

Whatever else you do, make this your top goal: Finish school! It's very difficult to get anywhere in the job market without graduating from high school. And while you're in school, cover the basics, such as math, reading, and writing. Solid grounding in these skills is important for almost every job.

SUSAN SMITH
1516 Sierra Way
Piedmont, California 97435
Telephone: (415) 486-3874

OBJECTIVE
Program development, coordination, and administration

Especially interested in a people-oriented organization where there is a need to assure broad cooperative effort through the use of sound planning and strong administrative and persuasive skills to achieve community goals.

MAJOR AREAS OF EXPERIENCE AND ABILITY
Budgeting and management for sound program development

With partner, established new association devoted to maximum personal development and self-realization for each of its members. Over a period of time, administered annual budget totaling $285,000. Jointly planned growth of group and related expenditures, investments, programs, and development of property holdings to realize current and long-term goals. As a result, holdings increased twenty-fold over this period, reserves invested increased 1,200%, and all major goals for members have been achieved. (A number have been exceeded.)

Purchasing to assure smooth flow of needed supplies and services

Usually alone (but in a strong give-and-take consultation with partner regarding major acquisitions), made most purchasing decisions to assure maximum production from available funds. Maintained continuous stock inventory to determine ongoing needs, selected suppliers, and assured proper disbursements to achieve a strong continuing line of credit while minimizing financing costs. Handled occasional "crash" needs so that no significant project was ever adversely affected by failure to mobilize necessary supplies, equipment, or services on time.

Personnel development and motivation

From the beginning, developed resources to assure maximum progress in achieving potential for development among all members of our group. Frequently engaged in intensive personnel counseling to achieve this. Sparked new community progress to help accomplish such results. Although arrangements with my partner gave me no say in selecting new members (I took them as they came), the results produced by this effort are a source of strong and continuing satisfaction to me. (See "specific results" below.)

Transportation management

Jointly with partner, determined transportation needs of our group and, in consultation with members, assured specific transportation equipment acquisitions over a broad range of types (including seagoing). Contracted for additional transportation when necessary. Assured maximum utilization of limited motor pool to meet often-conflicting requirements demanding arrival of the same vehicle at widely divergent points at the same moment. Negotiated resolution of such conflicts in the best interests of all concerned. In addition, arranged four major moves of all facilities, furnishings, and equipment to new locations—two across country.

Other functions performed

Duties periodically require my action in the following functional areas: crisis management ... proposal preparation ... political analysis ... nutrition ... recreation planning and administration ... stock market operations ... taxes ... building and grounds maintenance ... community organization ... social affairs administration (including VIP entertaining) ... catering ... landscaping (two awards for excellence) ... contract negotiations ... teaching ... and more.

Some specific results

Above experience gained in ten years devoted to family development and household management in partnership with my husband, Harvey Smith, who is equally responsible for results produced. Primary achievements: daughter Sue, 12, leading candidate for the U.S. Junior Olympics team in gymnastics; a lovely home in Piedmont (social center for area preteens). Secondary achievements: vacation home at Newport, Oregon (on the beach), and a cabin in Big Sur; president of Piedmont Junior High School PTA two years; organized successful citizen protest to stop incursion of Oakland commercialism on Piedmont area.

Personal data and other facts

Bachelor of arts (business administration), Cody College, Cody, California. Highly active in community affairs. Have learned that there is a spark of genius in almost everyone which, when nurtured, can flare into dramatic achievement.

Key Idea

Strong academic skills in reading, writing, and math will be valuable in almost any career path you choose.

Everyone has areas of strength as well as areas that could stand some improvement. Take an honest look at your academic skills, and don't be embarrassed to get help where you need it. A handicap in writing or reading or a difficulty with mathematical concepts could cost you a good job opportunity or hold you back in your future career. Consider school to be your *real* job right now, and make the most of it.

Also take advantage of extracurricular or school-related activities that tie into your career interests. School events, programs, and organizations offer ways to gain experience, skills, and knowledge in areas that may be useful later. Explore and experiment! Work with your guidance counselor to identify classes and activities that will give you the best background for your career path.

People Changing Careers

People are changing careers more frequently than ever, for a variety of reasons. Some people continue to search for more meaningful or higher-paying jobs; others are forced to seek new work because of layoffs, advancing technology, or changing employment trends. Whether a change occurs by choice or by force, it can be a challenging adjustment.

But it can also be a time for exciting growth and new opportunities. If you are making a major career change or looking for a new job, this is a time to carefully assess what you have liked in your previous work and what conditions or experiences you want to avoid. Do you have talents or skills that your previous job didn't give you a chance to use? Are you willing to relocate, invest in further training, or take a cut in salary?

It's important to consider what effects your changes will have on family and other people who are part of your life. Anticipating possible problems and making a plan with long-term objectives will help the transition from one job or career to another go more smoothly.

Emphasize the positive aspects of the work experience you have already gained, and keep in mind that employers are most interested in adaptive and transferable skills.

B·I·B·L·I·O·G·R·A·P·H·Y

Sources of Job Leads and Other Information

If you've been to a large bookstore lately, you've probably noticed that there are many books in the "career" section. Each year, there are more books published on this topic and, unfortunately, most of them are not very good. I have listed here resources that are of particular importance to you in your job search. Of course, I have included many of the books I have written and many that are published by JIST-it seemed only fair. Most are available from a bookstore or good library.

Career Planning, Job Seeking, Resumes, and Career Success

Job Seeking and Interviewing

The Very Quick Job Search: Get a Better Job in Half the Time! (2nd Edition) by J. Michael Farr. This is my most thorough job search book, and it includes lots of information on career planning and, of course, job seeking. This is the book I would recommend to a friend who is out of work if I had to recommend just one. (JIST)

The Quick Interview & Salary Negotiation Book: Dramatically Improve Your Interviewing Skills in Just a Few Hours! by J. Michael Farr. This is a substantial book with lots of information, but it's arranged so you can read the first section, then go out and do better in interviews the same day. (JIST)

Getting the Job You Really Want: A Step-by-Step Guide (3rd Edition) by J. Michael Farr. This one provides career planning and job search materials in a workbook format with lots of worksheets. It has sold more than 150,000 copies and counting. (JIST)

Career Satisfaction and Success: A Guide to Job and Personal Freedom by Bernard Haldane. This is a complete revision of a classic by one of the founders of the modern career planning movement. Not so much a job search book as a job success book. Contains solid information. (JIST)

Using the Internet and the World Wide Web in Your Job Search by Fred E. Jandt and Mary B. Nemnich. For new or experienced users of online computer services, this book gives lots of good information on finding job opportunities on the Web. (JIST)

The PIE Method for Career Success: A Unique Way to Find Your Ideal Job by Daniel Porot. Written by one of Europe's premier career consultants, this book presents powerful career planning and job seeking concepts in a visual and memorable way. (JIST)

Job Strategies for Professionals: A Survival Guide for Experienced White-Collar Workers by the U.S. Employment Service. Job search advice for professionals and managers who have lost their jobs. (JIST)

What Color Is Your Parachute? by Richard N. Bolles. This is the best-selling career planning book of all time, and the author continues to improve it. (Ten Speed Press)

The Complete Job Search Handbook: All the Skills You Need to Get Any Job, and Have a Good Time Doing It by Howard Figler. A very good book. (Henry Holt)

Who's Hiring Who? by Richard Lathrop. Another good book. (Ten Speed Press)

Job Hunters Sourcebook: Where to Find Employment Leads and Other Job Search Sources by Michelle LeCompte. (Gale Research)

Sweaty Palms Revised: The Neglected Art of Being Interviewed by Anthony Medley. (Ten Speed Press)

Dare to Change Your Job and Your Life by Carole Kanchier. Practical and motivating guidance on achieving career and personal growth and satisfaction. (JIST)

Resumes and Cover Letters

The Quick Resume & Cover Letter Book: Write and Use an Effective Resume in Only One Day by J. Michael Farr. Starting with an "instant" resume worksheet and basic formats that you can complete in an hour, this book takes you on a tour of everything you ever wanted to know about resumes and, more importantly, how to use them in your job search. (JIST)

The Resume Solution: How to Write (and Use) a Resume That Gets Results by David Swanson. Lots of good advice and examples for creating superior resumes. Very strong on design and layout, this book provides a step-by-step approach that is easy to follow. (JIST)

Gallery of Best Resumes: A Collection of Quality Resumes by Professional Resume Writers by David F. Noble. Advice and more than 200 examples from professional resume writers. With lots of variety in content and design, this is an excellent resource. I consider it the best resume "library" available. (JIST)

Gallery of Best Resumes for Two-Year Degree Graduates: A Special Collection of Quality Resumes by Professional Resume Writers by David F. Noble. A showcase of resumes written especially to help two-year degree graduates compete in the job market. (JIST)

Using WordPerfect in Your Job Search by David F. Noble. A unique and thorough book that reviews how to use the power of WordPerfect to create effective resumes, correspondence, and other job search documents. (JIST)

The Perfect Resume by Tom Jackson. (Doubleday)

Dynamite Cover Letters by Ron and Caryl Krannich. (Impact Publications)

Dynamite Resumes by Ron and Caryl Krannich. A good book. (Impact Publications)

The Damn Good Resume Guide by Yana Parker. Lots of good examples and advice. (Ten Speed Press)

Education, Self-Employment, and Starting a Business

Mind Your Own Business! Getting Started as an Entrepreneur by LaVerne Ludden and Bonnie Maitlen. A good book for those considering self-employment, with lots of good advice. (JIST)

Franchise Opportunities Handbook: A Complete Guide for People Who Want to Start Their Own Franchise by the U.S. Department of Commerce and LaVerne Ludden. Lists 1,500 franchise opportunities and information on selecting and financing a start-up. (JIST)

Back to School: A College Guide for Adults by LaVerne Ludden. Inside advice and valuable information for adults considering a return to school. (JIST)

Luddens' Adult Guide to Colleges and Universities by LaVerne Ludden and Marsha Ludden. Up-to-date information on more than 400 adult-friendly college and university programs in the U.S. (JIST)

The Career Connection for College Education: A Guide to College Education & Related Career Opportunities by Fred A. Rowe. Covers about 100 college majors and their related careers. (JIST)

The Career Connection for Technical Education: A Guide to Technical Training & Related Career Opportunities by Fred Rowe. Describes more than 60 technical education majors and the careers to which they lead. (JIST)

Information on Occupations and Industries

Occupational Outlook Handbook (OOH). Published every two years by the U.S. Department of Labor's Bureau of Labor Statistics, this book provides thorough descriptions of the 250 jobs that cover about 85 percent of the workforce, including information on skills required, working conditions, duties, qualifications, pay, and advancement potential. Very helpful for preparing for interviews by identifying key skills to emphasize. (U.S. Department of Labor; JIST publishes a reprint)

America's Top 300 Jobs. JIST's bookstore version of the OOH. The OOH itself is typically kept in the reference section of the library, but this version, which can often be checked out, allows you to access the same information at your leisure. (JIST)

Career Guide to America's Top Industries: Presenting Job Opportunities and Trends in All Major Industries (2nd Edition). Provides trends and other information on more than 40 major industries and summary data on many others. Includes details on employment projections, advancement opportunities, major trends, and a complete narrative description of each industry. (JIST)

The Complete Guide for Occupational Exploration (CGOE), edited by J. Michael Farr. Lists more than 12,000 job titles in a format that makes it easy to explore career alternatives or other jobs you may seek based on current skills. Jobs with similar characteristics are grouped together. The CGOE also cross-references to standard sources of additional information on the jobs it lists. (JIST)

The Enhanced Guide for Occupational Exploration (EGOE) (2nd Edition) compiled by Marilyn Maze and Donald Mayall. Using the same organizational structure as the CGOE, this book includes brief descriptions of about 2,800 jobs. Useful for career exploration, identifying skills used in previous jobs, researching new job targets, and preparing for interviews. (JIST)

151

Dictionary of Occupational Titles (DOT) (4th Edition Revised) by the U.S. Department of Labor. Provides descriptions for more than 12,000 jobs, covering virtually all jobs in our economy. This book can be used to identify jobs in different fields that use skills similar to those you have acquired in past jobs, identify key skills to emphasize in interviews, and much more. (U.S. Department of Labor, JIST publishes a reprint)

The Top Job Series. Each book in America's Top Jobs™ Series has a specific emphasis, providing thorough descriptions for the top jobs in a field, career planning and job search tips, plus details on growth projections, education required, and other data on 500 additional jobs. (JIST)

America's Fastest Growing Jobs

America's Federal Jobs

America's Top Office, Management, Sales & Professional Jobs

America's Top Medical, Education, & Human Services Jobs

America's Top Military Careers

America's Top Jobs™ for People Without College Degrees

America's Top Jobs™ for College Graduates

Dictionary of Occupational Terms: A Guide to the Special Language and Jargon of Hundreds of Careers by Nancy Shields. An interesting reference book that will answer most of your questions on more than 3,000 terms. (JIST)

✳ Information on Specific Organizations

Once you have a good idea of the industries, fields of work, and geographical areas in which you want to concentrate your job search, the next step is to locate companies that might employ people in your field. Several publications contain lists of companies by industry, location, size, and other defining characteristics. A few of them are discussed below.

The Job Hunter's Guide to 100 Great American Cities. Rather than concentrating on a particular locale, this guide gives the principal-area employers for 100 of America's largest cities. (Brattle Communications)

Macrae's State Industrial Directories. Published for 15 Northeastern states. Similar volumes are produced for other parts of the country by other publishers. Each book lists thousands of companies, concentrating almost exclusively on those that produce products rather than services. (Macrae)

National Business Telephone Directory. An alphabetical listing of companies across the United States, including addresses and phone numbers. This book includes many smaller firms. (Gale Research)

Thomas Register. Lists more than 100,000 companies across the country, including name, type of product made, and brand name of products. Catalogs provided by many of the companies are included. (Thomas)

America's Fastest Growing Employers. Lists more than 700 of the fastest growing companies in the country. (Bob Adams)

The Hidden Job Market: A Guide to America's 2000 Little-Known Fastest Growing High-Tech Companies. Concentrates on high-tech companies with good growth potential. (Peterson's Guides)

Dun & Bradstreet Million Dollar Directory. Provides information on 180,000 of the largest companies in the country, including type of business, number of employees, and sales volume. Also lists the company's top executives. (Dun & Bradstreet)

Standard & Poor's Register of Corporations, Directors and Executives. Information similar to that in Dun & Bradstreet's Million Dollar Directory. Also contains a listing of the parent companies of subsidiaries and the interlocking affiliations of directors. (Standard & Poor)

The Career Guide: Dun's Employment Opportunities Directory. Aimed specifically at the professional job seeker, this directory lists more than 5,000 major U.S. companies which plan to recruit in the coming year. Lists personnel directors and information about firms' career opportunities and benefits packages. (Dun)

There are many directories that give information about firms in particular industries. A few samples are listed below:

The Blue Book of Building and Construction

Directory of Advertising Agencies

Directory of Computer Dealers

McFadden American Bank Directory

Your local chamber of commerce and business associations may also publish directories listing companies in your area. These are available in libraries or by writing to individual associations. And, of course, the *Yellow Pages* provide local listings of government and business organizations for every section of the country.

Professional and Trade Associations

These associations offer another avenue for getting information about where to find the type of work you want to do. These associations:

▼ Help you identify areas where growth is occurring.

▼ Provide the names of firms that employ people in a specific type of work.

▼ Identify the best information sources for developments within the field.

▼ Provide more information on leads in small firms than directories.

▼ Publish newsletters or journals that provide information on companies needing increased staff in the near future.

153

Some publications that list trade and professional associations are listed below.

Encyclopedia of Associations. Lists more than 22,000 professional, trade, and other nonprofit organizations in the United States. (Gale Research)

Career Guide to Professional Associations. Describes more than 2,500 professional associations. The information is more specifically oriented to the job seeker than is the Encyclopedia of Associations, but this guide has not been updated since 1980, and some of the information may not be current. (Garrett Park Press)

Newspapers

Newspapers contain want ads and lots of other useful employment information. Articles about new or expanding companies can be valuable leads for new job possibilities.

If relocating is a possibility, look at newspapers from other areas. They can serve as a source of job leads as well as give you some idea of the job market. The major out-of-town newspapers are sold in most large cities and are also available in many public libraries.

Some newspapers—such as *The New York Times, The Chicago Tribune,* and *The Financial Times*—are national in scope. *The National Business Employment Weekly,* published by *The Wall Street Journal,* contains information of interest to professional job seekers.

Networking

Networking is an excellent way of gathering information about a particular field. It is one of the best ways to discover smaller companies, which often are not listed in directories.

Computer Software

Any good software store will carry programs to help you write a resume, organize your job leads and contacts, and create your correspondence. Some packages are also designed to provide "career counseling," occupational information, or advice on your job search. Some of these programs are good and some are not. If such programs interest you, consider them-but remember that few people get job offers while playing with their computers. You *do have to get interviews.*

A new release from JIST, titled *America's Top Jobs™ on CD-ROM!* is an excellent resource for career exploration and job seeking. It includes all the descriptions from the *Occupational Outlook Handbook* plus another 7,700 more specialized jobs. And it's only $24.95! It's a good example of what can be done with good software.